THE
Aligned
WOMAN'S WAY

VOLUME 2

DIANE MCKENDRICK
MICHELLE ANNE SAUNDERSON

First published by Ultimate World Publishing 2024
Copyright © 2024 Diane McKendrick

ISBN

Paperback: 978-1-923255-88-3
Ebook: 978-1-923255-89-0

Cover design: Ultimate World Publishing
Layout and typesetting: Ultimate World Publishing
Editor: Alex Floyd-Douglass

Ultimate World Publishing
Diamond Creek,
Victoria Australia 3089
www.writeabook.com.au

FROM THE AUTHOR

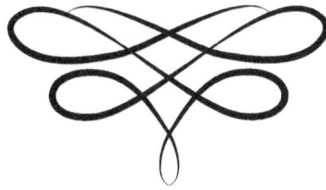

This book is the older, wiser, more mature sister of the *Aligned Woman's Way, Volume 1,* in which I and several co-authors shared our path to becoming the Aligned Woman in business.

Since publishing Volume 1, I've had so much life experience unfold, which rocked my world to the core, giving me a deeper, richer, more wholesome approach to life and business.

So, although I promised myself (similar to childbirth) that *'I'm never doing this again'* – I've found myself back for more.

Forgetting the pain of publishing a book and instead, focusing on the people it can support by sharing my deeper multidimensional message and gifts to the world and the opportunity to educate, inspire and empower even more people.

This book is bound to be the best yet, as I have my older sister, Michelle Anne, on board. Together, we have created something amazing for you!

Love,
Diane McKendrick

FROM THE AUTHOR

CONTENTS

INTRODUCTION

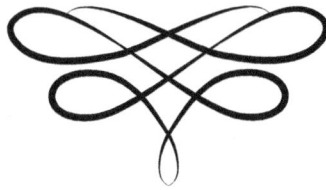

Ladies, let's get started!

It's time to cut the crap, do the thing and be the woman you were born to BE!

Most of you will know us by now. We are Michelle Anne and Diane from *Those2Sisters*.

We are real-life blood sisters; we have the same Mum and Dad.

Michelle, the older sister, an ex-police officer of 25 years who didn't-get-the-vax-so-got-the-sack, turned into a tree-hugging hippie and joined the business full-time in 2022.

Diane, the younger sister, was an extraordinary athlete in her younger years and is now the CEO of Overachievers Anonymous. A wild overachiever-turned-conscious-couch-potato – meaning she makes money and big business decisions while relaxing on the couch – Diane started the business in 2018.

This is our fourth best-selling book and our second together. We are well known for supporting high-achieving businesswomen on their journey to soulful success.

If you are reading this… We are talking to YOU!

This book holds the codes to timeless secrets and activations, rites of passage and initiations for businesswomen that aren't traditionally shared, talked about, or taught at business school and can't be bought at the shops – except for this book.

Our intention is that this book educates and enlightens you more than anything you have ever experienced over the years and that after reading it, you will feel a deep peace within, knowing you are in flow and in sync with your seasons and cycles.

The information and collective wisdom from ourselves and our co-authors come together in harmony to crack open your awareness and provide a framework, language, and community to discuss the seasons and cycles of life and how they not only affect your business but also alter your body and finances, relationships, connection to source, lifestyle, and identity.

This is for businesswomen of all ages so you can attune to your seasons and cycles and blend it with structure, strategy and systems to crack the code as to why something still feels like it is missing or why things still seem so hard or you're outwardly ok but still have that gnawing feeling in the pit of your stomach at 2am when you wake up to wee, and everything is quiet.

The Whisper is trying to be heard, but many of you are too busy being busy to hear her.

This book doesn't have to be read in order; however, with the elite intention of getting the most out of this book, I highly recommend diving into *The Aligned Woman's Way, Volume 1*, before consuming this one. There are some basic principles I share and discuss in depth during Volume 1 that will give you a solid foundation to build on.

You will hear from several of my clients as co-authors of this book, all of whom I have delicately hand-selected, knowing they have a wealth of embodied experience, knowledge, and practice and are devoted to the path of the *Aligned Woman*. They live their lives and run their businesses with a culmination of strategy, structure, and a heightened awareness of how the seasons and cycles of a woman's life organically blend with their successful business.

An Aligned Woman's Introduction to the Seasons and Cycles of Business

Use the energetics of business with the seasons and cycles of your life to break old, outdated paradigms and start EARNING and EVOLVING.

Become a pioneer in the industry and use our proven principles and examples in this book, combined with strategy, structure and your intuition, to achieve success beyond belief in ALL areas of your life!

Hear from other *Aligned Women* who will also share their journey and experience of personal seasons and cycles to cultivate their vision.

Create impact and income in an organic, professional and *Aligned* way.

Chapter One

COMING CLEAN: THE MUMMY MELTDOWN

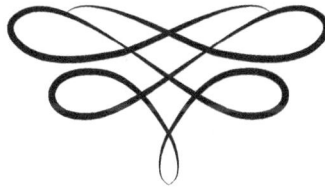

Similar to childbirth, after each book I published, I promised I would NEVER, EVER do it again.

The late nights, the self-doubt, the endless editing, the constant internal questioning, the fear of failure – I expected it would fade with each creation, but the truth is it gets more intense every time.

Putting more pressure on myself, with a wider reach, deeper engagement, and more people exposed to and invested in my message and mission, feels like an enormous amount of pressure. More depth, breadth and a whole lot of terrain and increasingly terrifying tax bills I am yet to acknowledge.

With the launch of each book (this is my fourth), my business has become more evolved, which means:

- More clients to serve
- More staff to supervise
- More money to manage
- More expenses to monitor
- More education to implement
- More experience to process

So similar to a fourth child… This fourth book has gotta fit in where I can fit it in. I am currently squished on a plane on my way to Tasmania. Tired, hungry, hot and would rather be catnapping, like the guy next to me in the checkered shirt… But my Whisper says, *'Write,'* so I listen. (Read more about connecting and hearing your whisper in Volume 1)

I honour my Whisper, get a second wind, and as most sleep, sip their wine, lose themselves in their murder mysteries, watch movies, scroll on their phones... I listen to my Whisper, and I GET STARTED.

Pausing momentarily to appreciate the rays of the setting sun shining through the window, I revert focus back to my laptop and keep going.

It dawns on me that as I type this paragraph, I notice the synchronicity of the timing of my trip to Tassie and the timing and topic of this book.

Seasons and cycles.

My sole purpose in travelling to Tasmania is for a photo shoot—a photo shoot for a consciously clean, professional skincare range whose company vision and devotion are to 'authentically ageing', not anti-aging or reverse-aging.

At 44 years old, with deep wrinkles and greying hair, I have been selected as the company's 'authentically aged model' for the founding photo shoot. The weight of this experience for me personally will be revealed in the following chapters as we dive deeper into questionable cultural collective beliefs around women and their roles and expectations in society as we age.

I am certain that it will speak to something within you and activate a deeper, more intimate, and vulnerable dialogue with yourself about your current season and cycle and your awareness and alignment with it.

What makes this trip even more special is that the photo shoot is for *She & I Skin Co,* which was birthed by my long-term clients Sarah and Ella Slatter, two sisters from Tasmania, whom we have worked with for the past few years.

Inspired at the *Energetics of Business Retreat* in Byron Bay, Australia, Sarah, a multi-business owner, contacted me a few days after her return during our 'After Retreat comeback process', which supports all our retreat attendees to come back from the magic of the Retreats and anchor their energetic high as their new normal. She said that after a process I had taken them through, and as a result of the space and people at the retreat, the idea landed that she had a dream to formulate her own consciously clean skincare range, based on her 12 years of experience working with skin in the beauty industry.

My response was simply, *'Let's get started!'*

I supported Sarah as her coach to overcome fear, uncertainty, and blocks and to start taking aligned actions. Soon into the process, Sarah decided to invite her younger sister, Ella, to join her. With Sarah leading the way, they have worked together to create a powerful, life-changing brand and product steeped in sisterhood, integrity, and embracing a woman's natural, radiant beauty with a consciously clean product that stands for so much more.

Another reason this was so fulfilling is that one of our leading referral partners is *Formulae Albury*. They are compounding pharmacists who specialise in women's hormones and have been Michelle Anne and my go-to for hormonal support through peri and peri-menopause.

So, I could confidently connect Sarah with *Formulae* and watch the magic unfold. If you are experiencing any symptoms of peri- or menopause, I would highly recommend *Formulae* for support. The team at *Formulae Albury* is professional, caring, and confident, and they have helped me and many of my clients (including Sarah and Ella) with female health. I will share their details later in the book.

It was so special to support Sarah and Ella and play the role of their coach through this. To add spice to life, as they were birthing this brand and product, Sarah gave birth to her second child.

Once again, this is a reminder of the seasons and cycles of a woman's life and how to juggle and balance motherhood, business ownership and community building. If you would like to order your own consciously clean skincare or book your hormone consultation with *Formulae*, their details are on the following pages:

SHE & I SKIN CO.

CONSCIOUSLY CLEAN

www.sheandiskinco.com.au

FORMULÆ

THE ART & SCIENCE OF COMPOUNDING

www.those2sisters.au/formulae-collab

Each book and each experience brings me closer to the core and offers up a more evolved experience and version of myself that gets unravelled through the process. There is a level of exposure and vulnerability that cannot be explained; it is only experienced.

I trust what is shared in this book through my storytelling and teaching style, combined with the words and wisdom of my co-authors, will ignite something in your soul that will stand the test of time.

It will open a conversation that initially may be uncomfortable and shocking to some. I ask you to stay open and curious through the pages of this book as we gently break generational patterns, discuss sensitive topics and lovingly crack open the crappy narratives and stories that trap women in a toxic cycle of comparison, sacrifice, attachment and obsession to youthfulness, looking and acting younger than we are.

Similar to labour, childbirth and motherhood, publishing a book is filled with the most intense divine dopamine hits and highs, yet is met on the other side with the harsh reality of days of depression, darkness, death of identity, constant questioning, tedious transitions, writer's block sprinkled with the loud and ever-present voice of the imposter.

Let's start with the latter – depression, darkness, death of identity and the missed rites of passage and evasive initiations that are stolen from women as we age.

Coming Clean: The Mummy Meltdown

My veil has recently been lifted in a distressing personal experience which I fondly call 'Mummy Meltdown'. A time in my life recently when I felt lost, lonely, isolated, defeated, frustrated, trapped, anxious and depressed for no understandable reason.

I've always been a good sleeper; randomly, I was suddenly waking up at 2am for months in a row with severe anxiety. Short of breath, sweating, hands squeezing into clenched fists, my mind whirling with intrusive thoughts like "I want to go for a drive and not return." I was obviously aware enough NOT to go for a drive and not come back; it was distressing waking night after night to that thought with not a single piece of evidence as to why I would be feeling something so extreme.

As a result of my restless nights, I would wake up in the morning exhausted, feeling sluggish and tired; my head ached daily as what once was easy became almost impossible. The day-to-day running of the household, which I used to manage with ease and finesse, all of a sudden weighed heavily on me. Likewise, business began to feel hard and stressful. The easiest of tasks felt like massive mountains, and each night, I fell into bed, barely recognising myself.

My self-talk slowly became peppered with mini bombs waiting to go off, the main one being, *'What's wrong with me?'* on repeat on a loop in my head.

A once bright, active, capable mum and businesswoman struggling behind closed doors to keep it together. The slow and subtleness of this is like a stealth ninja in the night.

Adding to the fire, and probably the most confusing and painful part, is that there was absolutely no reason for me to feel like this.

I was fit and healthy, exercising daily and eating well, no longer drinking alcohol.

Finances were structured, organised and safe, with income increasing and expenses decreasing.

I had (and still have) a wonderful, supportive, caring, aware partner and two healthy, albeit challenging, children. I also had extended family close by, who were all very hands-on and supportive.

I purposefully woke up every day to serve in a business that I hand-built brick by brick with my older sister. I've actualised my childhood dreams of becoming a Best-Selling Author and having nearly 200 podcasts published.

We have the best clients and containers in the world, and they fill me with joy and adventure every day.

I travel when I want, holiday with my family, and go on regular girls' trips away. I live the lifestyle on my vision board from five years ago.

I feel deep *Alignment* in all areas of my life, running and attending my online signature course, *The Aligned Woman Academy*, every month for myself and my clients.

I created the *Alignment Archetype* quiz as part of Volume 1 and would do this regularly to keep myself in check. Before reading any further, I invite you to go and do the quiz for yourself so you can get your starting point.

We get incredibly positive feedback from this quiz, with many clients saying that simply completing the quiz seems to shift something immediately for them.

You can access it HERE

So there was NO visible or valid reason I was experiencing this inner turmoil, which made me feel like something was wrong with me, like a fraud, and I didn't tell anyone about it, convincing myself, *'This will pass.'*

It didn't pass – it got worse.

The longer it went on, the worse it got. I started having heart palpitations, dizzy spells, horrific nightmares that left me in night sweats and still reeling from them the day after.

I was managing through my days and hadn't told anyone how I was feeling. Like so many women, I couldn't explain it. I simply got on with it like we have been taught. Until one night, it all came to a head.

I was putting my kids to bed, and as usual, they were not keen or obliging, resisting the transition to winding down, not wanting to switch off, slow down and sleep. The usual performance and clever procrastination and distraction techniques drawing out the process, which, let's face it, is frustrating and annoying, but I can usually deal with it fine, remain regulated, calm and support them to sleep.

This one night – I snapped.

And I mean, really lost it. Usually, when that happens, I yell and scream, carrying on like a pork chop, but this time, something was different. I rolled over, and I sobbed. I cried, cried and cried for hours. I ended up fitfully sleeping on the couch, which I have never done, tossing and turning. By the morning, I couldn't hold it in any longer. A painful and private moment for us Mums, which is rarely shared and definitely NOT talked about.

My husband was in the kitchen cooking breakfast and preparing my coffee, making kids' lunches… and everything else that happens in a family kitchen each morning. As he stood in the kitchen beside the sizzling eggs and brewing coffee, I stumbled into the kitchen and crumbled in his arms. Sobbing, crying, coming clean about how I had been feeling and the guilt associated with it because I had *'the perfect life'*.

Through the snot, tears and build-up of uncertainty and fear, I blurted it all out. Somehow, that amazing man managed to hold me, cook the eggs, feed the cat, prepare the kids' lunches, and make me feel held, supported and seen.

Coming Clean: The Mummy Meltdown

This was the start of a very challenging time for me, and although sharing to this depth and vulnerability has me feel like I'm going to 😤 and 🙈 at the same time, it was my first introduction (at 44 years old) to the natural seasons and cycles of a woman's life and how the rites of passages, feelings, emotions and physical changes have been overlooked, dismissed and lost in a world that fantasies fast, quick fixes and is obsessed with surface level success and prolonged physical beauty.

The days that followed were hectic. I needed to get away to reset but had enormous unexplained anxiety. Terrified to leave the house, terrified to stay. After chatting with my husband, Gus, it took all of my courage to pack a few of my things and head to the coast to stay with family so I could take some time and get a break.

Anxiety quickly turned to guilt and abandonment, feeling guilty about having to take time for myself and feeling like I was abandoning my family for my own mental health. It was midweek, the kids had sports, my husband had work, and I felt the burden of leaving like a heavy weight on my chest. I could barely breathe during the whole car trip to the coast.

Naturally, I knew myself to be someone who thrives, flourishes and celebrates time on my own. So, it was shocking to me to notice that this time, something was very different. No responsibilities, no routine, no expectations, no identity, no jobs, something when I was feeling fine, I would be doing cartwheels and singing from the rooftop, but for some random reason simply the thought of this dedicated time and space triggered a stress and panic response, which I had never experienced.

My Whisper was clear: *'Get away, take time on my own,'* simultaneously, the gift of time and space to heal and feel was petrifying.

Finally, after years of relentless devotion to my family, business, health, personal development and hectic emotional healing, I had the thing that many of us dream of and 'think' we want…

A few days dedicated 100% TO ME.

There is no outcome or expectation required, no schedules or time constraints, no financial worries or chores, no errands to run, no pickup or drop-offs, no washing, meal prep, or shopping.

Like I said. Dream days.

My mind swirled, confused, wondering why it felt so terrifying and hard to leave suddenly.

Usually a grounded, confident, clever person, the intense shakiness I was feeling, I could NOT shift and was not a familiar part of who I was and how I 'did life'.

I craved familiarity, routine, and some certainty – something to cling to and feel safe, hoping that all these intense, wild, and unfamiliar emotions and feelings would make some sense.

It got worse before it got better. Even as I type this (on the plane on the way home from Tassie this time), I'm unsure if I will share the above; the vulnerability hangover is in full swing already.

Coming Clean: The Mummy Meltdown

But do you know what? My whisper says, *'Share it.'*

As a collective, we need to stop pretending everything's okay, stop posting on social media the highlight reel of life and share both sides, in a way that feels authentic, real and safe for you.

I feel I have a moral obligation to women to share the truth and my experience above to remind each of us (including myself) that pain has a purpose.

I have the tenancy and skill to skip over the painful parts like a stealth ninja, and as a world-class life coach for businesswomen, I move myself and my clients very effectively to the desired outcome and result.

Over the few days away, diving into the darkness and depths of myself, I shared on social media in real time the struggle I was experiencing. I stopped all other advertising and scheduling; I simply showed up when I wanted with the truth of my heart and experience, sharing the internal chaos and questioning. I looked and sounded terrible after not sleeping well for months, coupled with waves of uncontrollable crying at any moment.

Using my own modality, *Those2Sisters Divine Hypnotics*, to delve deep into my psyche and rewire and reconnect, it became clear there was a lot of unprocessed grief sitting in my system.

Weirdly enough, as I was moving through, I had this unusual feeling that it wasn't my grief; it didn't make sense. I had nothing to be sad about. With further gentle exploration and self-direction, I uncovered it was lineage grief from ancestors and let me tell you, it was hectic.

This is another topic I won't dive into during this book; however, if you experience or feel anything I have explained so far and can't find your answers, keep this possibility under your cap. If you would like to explore this topic further, you can listen to episode #174 of the Aligned Woman's Way podcast series.

By the time I came home a few days later, I definitely felt better; however, the anxiety turned to fear about coming home and not being able to cope again. Feeling an unexplainable distance from my closest friends and family, I wondered again, *'Am I going crazy?'*

Upon returning home, I had the capacity to manage basic daily tasks again. Something seemed instinctually different. Nothing made sense anymore; I felt listless and disconnected, numb to things that used to excite me. Again, the pages of my journal were filled with *'What's wrong with me? Am I going crazy?'*

Everything was changing without my understanding; my body started to change, my relationship with my kids and husband morphed, and once again, I was left reeling, confused and questioning it all.

As I kept showing up and sharing with real, raw authenticity, a few older ladies reached out, mentioning they had been through similar experiences and had I considered Perimenopause.

Coming Clean: The Mummy Meltdown

At 44, I received my first introduction to the sacred, necessary, and life-altering seasons and cycles of a woman's life...

After researching and reaching out to other women in my community who specialise in this topic and have similar embodied experiences, EVERYTHING STARTED TO MAKE SENSE.

After some time at the bottom of the barrel for no apparent reason, it was time to be supported, seen, held and honoured by the women in my extended community who so solidly took my hand and held my heart through this process.

They listened, laughed, cried, and supported me in honouring and wholeheartedly sharing my experience with the intention of finding my own answers.

They gave me a framework, language and community to discuss and share the natural seasons and cycles of a woman's life and how to overcome the shame and secrecy of a stolen and dismissed rite of passage into authentically ageing women in society and business.

There is so much sitting under the surface collectively for women. Culturally, many of us have been indoctrinated into subtly believing that women lose their value in society as they age. As our hair greys, our wrinkles deepen, our bodies soften, and our energy shifts from spring to winter, we somehow become less important and valuable in society.

There are multi-million dollar industries based on this misled truth and women as a collective feeling 'less than' as we age and life moves from fast pace, hustle, achievement and success to a much softer, slower pace…

If you struggle to believe this, and it's a hard pill to swallow (which it was and still sometimes is for me), imagine stopping dying your hair, getting Botox and embracing your current season and cycle.

It is not an overnight change, but it could be. It was shocking to me the first time I explored this, and as mentioned at the beginning of this chapter, I am certain that it will speak to something within you and activate a deeper, more intimate and vulnerable dialogue with yourself about your current season and cycle and your awareness and alignment to it.

My wish is that my experience and the collective wisdom from my co-authors and *Soul Sisters,* come together and land in your world to crack open your heart and awareness on how seasons and cycles of life and business work. They are not just responsible for moods, thoughts, feelings, emotions, changed connection to the people and ideas closest and truest to you but to simultaneously educate and empower women to notice and embrace how these next stages of a woman's life wildly alter her business, body, brain, finances, the way she relates to herself, her children and ultimately, her identity and therefore, entire life.

It's been a wild ride, and I know it may have been a wild one for you. And if not, sure enough, as the sun rises tomorrow, there will be some point in the next several years when the information in this book or a woman in this book will be an anchor point for you to shine the light when everything else seems really dark.

What matters most is not how you look, how many dollars your business makes, what car you drive, or how many followers you have; it's how you feel and navigate the dark times, the winter seasons that no one speaks of, the times when nothing makes sense anymore and everything seems to be in a cycle of decay, like business, body, products, services, and relationships.

It is the ending of an era that you have poured your heart and soul into. Ensure you have safety nets in place in your business to support the seasons and cycles of your life so you can take the time you need to rest, reset, recalibrate, and re-choose.

Now, let's dive in!

Chapter Two

MAKING SENSE
OF IT ALL

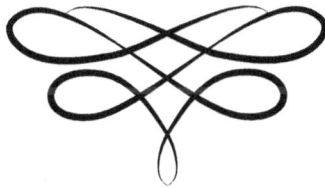

So now I have come clean and bared my tender heart to you all with the intention of sharing my vulnerabilities so you know that you're not on your own, you're not going crazy, and there is nothing wrong with you; it's time to backtrack a little bit to ensure you are prepped and ready for the next step in the journey of the *Aligned Woman's Way*.

In Volume 1, we first get clear on your starting point by using the *Archetypes Quiz*. If you haven't paused reading to do it, here is the link again.

We explained your *Daily Deep Dive* and gave journal prompts as your personal guide to uplevel your experience and make it easy and effortless for you. Many of you reported back to us that this process stopped the confusion, overwhelm and erratic action or non-action and gave you the clarity to take inspired action on a day-to-day basis.

We made the distinction between the voice of your *Whisper* and the voice of your *Wounding*, explained how to discern where the voices in your head come from – and gave some ideas and exercises on how to relate to them differently so you can stop pinballing through life doing lots but not getting much done.

Ladies from all over the world now use this framework in their daily language and comment that the explanation and exercises in Volume 1 have given them a complete 180-degree turn in their lives. They no longer feel tormented and torn apart by the voice in their head but are able to feel confident and clear-headed and take inspired action accordingly.

From there, we discussed your *Alignment Audit* and offered complimentary meditations, hypnosis and visual models to support your internal shift and transformation without you having to do more.

Our readers and clients gave us feedback that our *Alignment Audit* supported them in getting shit done without the panic, urgency, rush and overwhelm.

So, before moving on, my invitation is to revisit Volume 1 and ensure you have the basic groundings upon which to build. This book can be purchased from our website at *www.those2sisters.com*

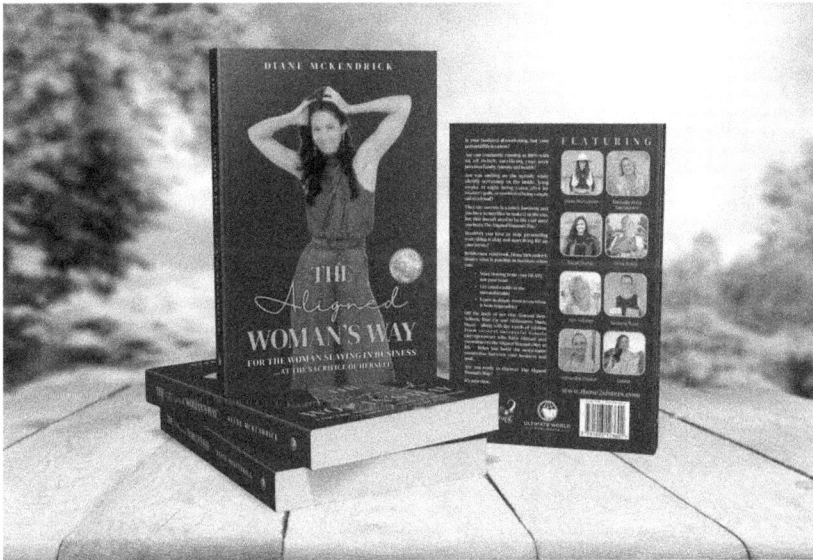

If you already have a copy, pull it out and keep it beside you as you read through. The format I intentionally used for Volume 1 was 'journal style,' so there are plenty of places to write your answers, fill out your journal prompts, draw and colour on the diagrams, and really make it your own living, breathing book bestie that gets so well used it has earmarked pages, highlighted paragraphs, your handwriting through it and seconds as a personal journal as you journey through the pages.

To make it easy for you, here is a checklist of basic principles before we move into education and content in *Volume 2, Seasons and Cycles*.

- [ ] Archetype Quiz

- [ ] Daily Deep Dive

- [ ] Attuned to your Whisper

- [ ] Alignment Audit

Aligned
WOMAN'S WAY

Okay, so now we've got the logistics done, let's get down to business.

In this chapter, it is my intention to share the lessons, learnings and wisdom I gathered from the challenging *Mummy Meltdown* I shared earlier.

I have researched, dreamt, prayed, interviewed people, journaled, laughed and cried through the process. This chapter is dedicated to sharing my learnings, education and hopefully inspiration with my fellow business mums on the rollercoaster of organic, natural seasons and cycles of a woman's life.

These cycles impact everything from how we feel to what we look like, what we think, how we create, and who we are as individuals and as a community.

I will break down my personal research, interviews, lessons, and learnings with the intention of giving language, framework, education, awareness, and inspiration to other women who might be feeling lost, confused, isolated, and like they don't know who they are anymore.

A mammoth task for one chapter, right?

My chapters and content will be followed up by my co-authors, who will share their journey in life and business, and you will notice similarities through their personal stories.

For many of my co-authors, this is the first time they have shared personal, vulnerable and private life experiences, which showcases the authenticity and depth of challenge we all experience at some point in our lives, which is less shared and talked about than the success, celebrations and wins.

I was deeply moved while reading their chapters and simultaneously cherished and was challenged by the roller coaster ride. Sobbing tears one minute and laughing uncontrollably with excitement the next. I'm so grateful I get front-row seats right beside each of these incredible ladies as they ride the rollercoaster of seasons and cycles of life and business.

As my business started to thrive and I transformed from the little shy girl from Ipswich to a well-known, world-class life coach for businesswomen, speaking on stages globally and coaching women all around the world, I watched in awe as they did the work within our containers and completely changed their lives from the inside out.

In addition to my services, I started an audio hypnosis library to support my clients' growth and transformation. I used their real-life, personal rollercoaster moments to customise the hypnosis and help them overcome the pattern or behaviour blocking or limiting them.

It was a wild ride to witness more and more women (who I used to be intimidated by) step into my containers, deeply trusting themselves and trusting me as their coach and community.

People get fast, long-term and sustainable results when they work with us because when you say YES to our signature online course, *The Aligned Woman Academy* or do what it takes to attend *Those2Sisters Retreats*, your timeline changes and what becomes possible amplifies.

We have had ladies have wild, long-term, and sustainable success in ALL areas of their lives. In our online course and retreats, we break it down into six main areas of life.

BODY: Alice lost 45kg after her first retreat and kept it off. Nicole stopped drinking coffee and has been clear for over a year. Kelli stopped drinking alcohol every night and has lost 15kg to date. She walks every day and has started drinking morning gut health tonics.

FINANCE: Sally, a mother of two, owns two businesses where she only works three hours a week and earns over $100k a year. Michelle left her job in the Police and made her whole annual salary in one day.

RELATIONSHIPS: Kathy found her dream partner and quit her job in childcare to travel around Australia in her camper van with her beloved. She blogs and holds relationship workshops on their travels. Gwen cut soul contracts with an ex-partner who had been tormenting her for years and now sets boundaries, feels grounded and is confident in her interactions with him. Betty healed her relationship with her estranged son.

SPIRITUALITY: We have had countless calls, messages and moments of witnessing women from all over the world have their 'moment' and, for moments, be speechless with the shift they experience once they are reconnected to source energy or what they believe is bigger than themselves.

SOUL PURPOSE: Suzanne has actualised her dream of holding her own retreats, coaching and mentoring packages for people experiencing grief. Hayley started her podcast and blogging after the *Soul Purpose* process in AWA, and *Those2Tassie (Tasmania) Sisters* co-founded and launched their consciously clean skincare range.

LIFESTYLE: Every morning, I wake up to live the life I once dreamed of. I go for my morning walk and reply to my hand-selected 1:1 clients, who are women all living their dream lifestyles. My life is delicately curated day by day as we show you how to design your days around your highest values and priorities and how to make money by doing what you love with who you love. We have ladies living their dream lifestyles, and it's deeply inspiring—and a great reminder to keep going!

After coaching these superstars in potent, powerful co-creation between client and coach, I closely observed and started recording their rituals of success. I was laser-focused on noticing their patterns of behaviour, language, recurring thought patterns, actions, or inactions. I grouped these patterns/ people into four categories. With this research, I created my own Intellectual Property, which I coined *'The Life Cycle of Business'*.

This framework alone has supported Michelle, me, and hundreds of women through the seasons and cycles of business.

Those 2 Sisters

Cycle of Business

Seed
"She's just starting out"

Sapling
"She pops through"

Those 2 Sisters

Lotus
"She takes up space"

Blossom
"She blooms"

"Everything is where it needs to be"

SEED: SHE'S JUST STARTING OUT

CHARACTERISTIC	Just starting out. Has an idea/vision but not sure what to do. No systems yet.
VISION	Has a vision but doesn't know how.
WORK ETHIC	Extreme – either a million miles an hour or... Nothing. On or off.
MONEY	Struggles to receive and doesn't have bank accounts or bookkeeping set up.
SYSTEMS	No systems or website.
FUNNEL	Either it's scattered or non-existent.
STRUCTURE	What's that?
TIME	Frenetic, trying to fit it all in. Still cleaning, shopping and being everything to everyone.
FEELING	Ambitious, hopeful and excited. A little nervous.
THOUGHTS	*'I've got so much to do and I don't know where to start.'*
CHALLENGES	Limiting beliefs and lack of confidence.
FOCUS 4	Rituals & Routines, Time Management, Creating a Clear Offer, Confidence.

Given the right environment, the seed will flourish into a Sapling:

The 4 most important things a SEED needs to move to SAPLING IS:

- Rituals & Routines
- Time Management
- Clear Offer
- Confidence

Making Sense of It All

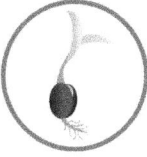

SAPLING : SHE POPS THROUGH

CHARACTERISTIC	Starting to get some traction, seeing a difference.
VISION	Strength in her vision and it's driving her, she is starting to be the 'embodiment' of the work but it's still an effort. Trying really hard.
WORK ETHIC	Still flapping and going pretty hard and fast. Saying YES to opportunities.
MONEY	It's slowed down again, but it's easier to come by. Random amounts are starting to land. A little stress is starting to build as she madly researches bank accounts, accountants, and bookkeepers.
SYSTEMS	Starting the process of thinking about, learning, and researching which systems will be best suited for her style of business. Nervous about the outlay as there's no guarantee it will come back. 'I can't afford it' thoughts.
FUNNEL	Barebones are in place. Foundations are being built. There's still some confusion, but solid riverbanks are forming (you just don't know it yet).
STRUCTURE	Slowly taking place, but it's more chaotic than calm at the moment.
TIME	A blend between focus and frenetic energy. Getting more moments of clarity.
FEELING	Highest of highs and lowest of lows (within 5 minutes of each other).
THOUGHTS	*'I'm doing this. I'm really doing this... Am I REALLY doing this?'*
CHALLENGES	Frenetic energy.
FOCUS 4	Discern your YES/NO's, outsource as much as you can, create a safe structured space for your money to come to play, and choose your sacred systems.

Given the right environment, the sapling will flourish into a blossom:
The 4 most important things a SAPLING needs to move to a BLOSSOM are:
- Discern your YES/NOs.
- Outsource as much as you can.
- Create a safe structured space for your money to come to play.
- Choose your sacred systems.

BLOSSOM : SHE BLOOMS

CHARACTERISTIC	Confidence in herself and product or offers.
VISION	Rock-solid and evolving.
WORK ETHIC	Starting to set and hold boundaries in business as well as in personal life.
MONEY	Money is starting to flow and has a home, structure and organisation. Still learning.
SYSTEMS	Implementing slowly. The most important being done 1st and learning how to use them.
FUNNEL	Starting to look like a piece of art. Falling into place. Simple, clear and strategic with space for flow and intuition.
STRUCTURE	Being guided strongly by a sense of structure (it can become a trap and make you robotic - be wary). You can grip to it to feel a sense of safety and it can have you become stagnant.
TIME	Structured with SPACE. A deep sense of accomplishment.
FEELING	This is fun and it's starting to get easier.
THOUGHTS	*'I've found myself a job. My days have started to become boring. The excitement has started to wane.'*
CHALLENGES	Trapped by structure and becoming stagnant.
FOCUS 4	Sacred Sales, Customer relationships and nurturing, self-care.

Given the right environment, the blossom will flourish into a lotus:

The 4 most important things a BLOSSOM needs to move to a LOTUS is:

- Sacred Sales
- Customer relationships
- Nurturing
- Self-care

LOTUS: SHE TAKES UP SPACE

CHARACTERISTIC	Confident, Trusting, Abundant, Flowing, Graceful, Secure.
VISION	Embody it most days.
WORK ETHIC	Solid and sturdy, flowing.
MONEY	Loads of it and a great relationship to it.
SYSTEMS	Sturdy and being audited/refined.
FUNNEL	Clear, concise and exciting to you.
STRUCTURE	Functional and free.
TIME	Getting your time back as you have outsourced and have a team on board.
FEELING	Fulfilled, content and ready to shed and start the cycle again.
THOUGHTS	*'How does it get any better than this?'*
CHALLENGES	Getting ready for the cycle to start again. Mental game/grief of letting go of past lessons and reference points. Embracing the void, scarcity.
FOCUS 4	Trust, resetting your financial thermostat, maintaining abundant mindset, reflection/radical acceptance.

Given the right environment, the blossom will flourish into a lotus:

The Lotus will eventually cycle back into a seed. In the meantime the Lotus needs to:

- Trust
- Resetting your financial thermostat
- Maintaining abundant mindset
- Reflection/radical acceptance

This model has supported Michelle, me, and many of our clients numerous times in resetting, recalibrating, and refocusing. The first step is to determine where you currently are in your business and then use *Focus4* to tell you exactly what you need to do to move to the next level.

For example, when someone is a Seed, it's a requirement to be disciplined to your calendar, whereas in contrast, by the time you're a Lotus, if you are too disciplined and a robot to your calendar, it will stifle your creativity and flow.

People think the aim of the game is to become the Lotus. This is partly true, the part most aren't aware of and is exactly what this book is about…

What happens after you have made it to the top?

That's right. Death, decay, letting go, starting again, transformation – this is the dark part people don't like to talk about; some call it the *'dark night of the soul',* and my co-author, Marissa, explains it beautifully in her chapter.

What happens is that you start out on the journey as a piddly little seed, a weak plant that is easily upheaved or blown over. Each time through the cycle, you become a stronger seed until you have moved through it many times, and you are an Oak Tree seed.

Once that seed is planted, it grows big, bold and deep. It grows branches and shade for others around it and drops its own seeds within the community. It is hard to knock over and has a solid foundation and presence.

Making Sense of It All

Same process, different depth.

My clients rave about the clarity this framework gifts them and, therefore, the focus and momentum in their life and business. With that as feedback, I decided to add it into this book for you all to experience.

I created this concept in about 2021, during COVID-19, as I was crisis coaching many business owners and parents through the hardships of uncertainty and fear of what was unfolding in the world.

So, although I was very ignorant about the in-depth details of seasons and cycles in a woman's life, I wasn't completely unaware or blind to them.

I knew the basics, what society teaches us and what people talk about, possibly similar to the knowledge most people in this culture understand.

Little girls become young teenagers, which is signified by the start of menstruation; teenagers become young ladies in their 20s or 30s – young ladies spend the 1st several years trying not to get pregnant, and then the internal clock starts ticking, young ladies become older ladies and it switches from trying not to get pregnant to trying to get pregnant and have babies and become mothers, of which is the BIGGEST shock of all…

Then the kids grow up and move out – young ladies turn into old ladies and stop menstruating, which is rarely talked about. But, as with the start of menstruation, labour and childbirth, often people are very forthcoming with the traumatic stories and on with life you go.

So little girls grow up into mothers and old ladies without much of a thought for what it means, who we are, what we become or even who the heck we really are as our hormones rage, surge and play havoc with our perfectly curated lies, I mean lives.

Often colliding with the raging, surging hormones of our children, who often are going through their own shifts and changes at the same time as the mother. Now, this… without awareness and support, can be a battlefield for families.

I hadn't really thought or learned much more about it until I was forced through my own confusing and terrifying experience, which I shared in Chapter 1.

In my first session with Lyndsee Cunningham from *Held By Lyndsee*, I was absolutely mind-blown by how much empowerment I gained from Lyndsee's holding a no-judgment space for me. She educated and empowered me and held me when I couldn't do it for myself when I felt confused, defeated, isolated and like I was going crazy.

Lyndsee is a certified guide of *Seasons of Matrescence*™, supporting women to navigate the change and seasons of life and motherhood.

Matrescence™ is a body of work created by Nikki McCahon and is the journey to and through motherhood. It is a universal, individual, and unique experience for each woman; it is ongoing and cyclical with no end goal, showing us that we are always re-negotiating our values, identity, and experiences as women as we grow beside our children and business. As our children or businesses grow through their own stages, we will also be renegotiating who we are, what is important to us and how we make meaning in our lives.

Though using Nikki McCahon's body of work, *Matrescence*™, Lyndsee, a certified practitioner, was able to support me to reorientate me by mapping the aligning seasons and the various energies so I could understand and re-orientate me first and, therefore, my business to the present season and cycle.

Using this education empowered me to look inward and cultivate self-compassion and gave me a language and framework to understand what was happening to me so I could normalise my experience, centre myself and share it wIth you.

There is a potent and powerful podcast where I interview Lyndsee; you can listen to it on *Spotify* on Episode 176 of *The Aligned Woman's Way*. It is aptly called, *'Ever secretly thought, am I going crazy?'*

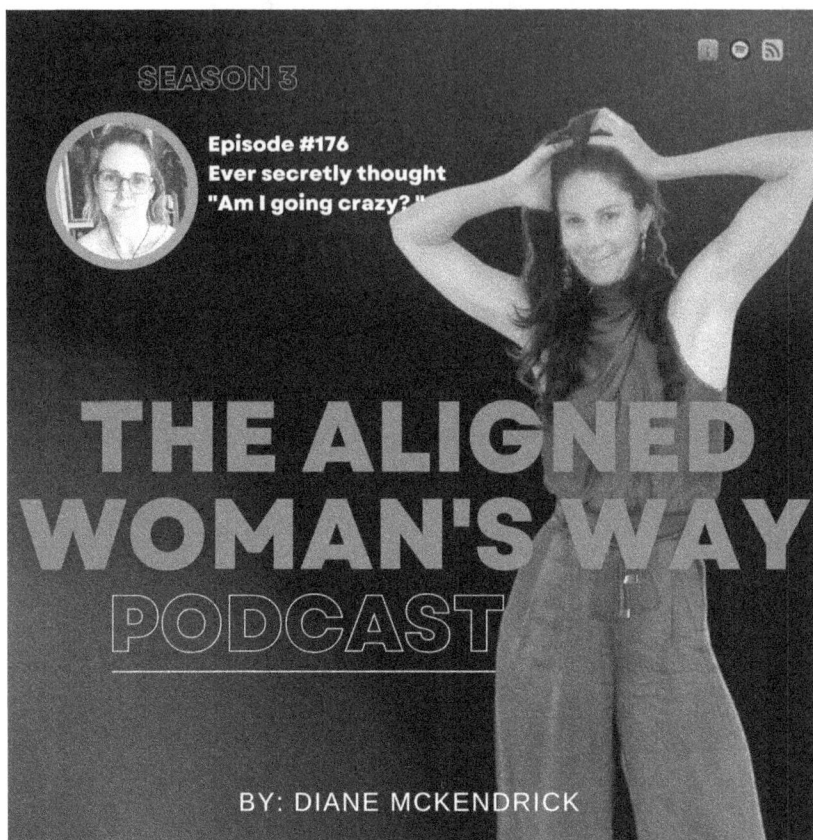

This podcast goes into greater detail about the experience and how I was able to move through it because of the support, awareness, information, and understanding that nothing was wrong with me, but it was a very normal and important part of the SEASON I was/am in. With the click of the fingers, I went from terrified and tormented to empowered and excited.

I learnt about the four main cycles of a woman's life:

Making Sense of It All

1. MAIDEN
2. MOTHER
3. MAGA
4. CRONE

As I dove deep into each cycle and learnt more about how I was feeling and what I was experiencing, it all seemed to make so much more sense.

Unfortunately, it came to my awareness that our culture seems to be fixated and obsessed with the Maiden, splits and sacrifices the Mother, ignores the Maga and casts aside the Crone.

I was shocked to notice that weaved into the tapestry of our culture as a collective, we fixate on the youthful looks, young energy and radiant beauty of our Maidens (before motherhood).

Because of this, many Maidens fall victim to feelings of inadequacy. Constant feelings of being fundamentally flawed, never enough, urgency, rush and overwhelm and an unhealthy obsession with external looks and weight lead to emotional dysregulation and an era of young women who are disempowered, working too hard to prove themselves and on a never-ending cycle of anxiety and frustration.

On the journey into motherhood, our focus shifts to survival, the mother splitting herself into different identities, sacrificing her body and identity and becoming a mother with little to no support. This leads to feelings of resentment, isolation and loneliness, leaving mothers feeling scattered, exhausted, and running on empty with not much more to give.

As our kids, pets, or business grows and they don't need us to mother/nurture them anymore, she starts to move into the perimenopausal stage. It's like she is of less value and importance to society and is ignored as she no longer has her youthful good looks and vitality, or her main role and identity as a mother is no longer required.

Often, by this stage, she feels invisible and ignored by society. This can lead to feelings of abandonment, frustration, and confusion, which, unmonitored or supported, can turn into depression...

WITHOUT EVEN REALISING IT!

By the time she moves into full menopause, her looks, body, and identity take another thrashing. With greying hair and wrinkling skin, it is like society casts her aside unless she maintains a certain standard to look and act a certain way (like a maiden).

This leads to feelings of inadequacy, isolation, and disconnection and can be very damaging to her self-worth and self-esteem and the way she occupies space in the world.

The above is only a HALF TRUTH; it's what we have been subtly led to believe as a society. The deeper I dove, the more I noticed it weaved into the fabric of society, and the subtle shifts, changes, and transitions into each stage go unnoticed, uncelebrated and without support.

NO WONDER I WAS FEELING SO BLAH... And maybe you are, too.

Making Sense of It All

It's also important to remember as we journey through the seasons and cycles of a woman's life that change, which is inevitable, is one of the most dysregulating things to our central nervous system. To date, many of us have not been seen, supported, and acknowledged through the most massive and disruptive changes of our lives.

The first step to change is awareness, so keep reading along. I promise you that by the end of the book, it will all make much more sense. You will better understand what season and cycle you are navigating and some crucial points to support you. You also have a built-in community here at *Those2Sisters* of women who speak this language and are here every step of the way.

It is time to rewrite this narrative and change the subliminal belief, pull in the other side of the coin and become aware of what gifts are here for us in each of these cycles.

The Maiden is full of vibrant young energy, youthful beauty and a breath of fresh air.

The Mother is a force to be reckoned with, showing herself that she is capable of more than she ever imagined, learning how to feel the full spectrum of emotions and feelings and surprisingly feel opposing feelings at once. E.g. be so frustrated, exhausted and defeated with the lack of sleep and what's required of her body as a mother and simultaneously feel deep, unconditional love for her child/ren.

The becoming of a Maga: She steps into the era of medicine woman with more space, returning to nurturing herself and sharing her wisdom.

Our beautiful Crones can celebrate and be celebrated as she enters her golden years.

If the woman is seen and supported through the above transitions, she will lead a very fulfilled, exciting, powerful life in which we are a force to be reckoned with as a collective.

But wait, there is more…

In addition to this, I learnt more about the seasons of a woman's life. Summer, Winter, Autumn, and Spring are things I thought were exclusive to the weather. Well, it turns out each of us is moving through seasons at each moment of our lives, and if you are unaware like I was, fighting against it, life and business will be HARD!

If you can honour and flow with your organic, natural season and cycle and align your behaviour, feelings, and expectations within your business with your current internal season, things will flourish in perfect time.

It is my intention that, with this book and the words and examples from my co-authors, you will be well-equipped to ride the rollercoaster of seasons and cycles of life.

You will feel educated and empowered to understand what is happening within your body and honour your current season.

To acknowledge and hold space for other women moving through the cycles with love and compassion and in a place of no judgement and expectation.

And in doing that, gift yourself the same love, compassion, no judgement and expectation.

MICHELLE ANNE

❝ Allowing and trusting is true courage. ❞

www.those2sisters.com

Chapter Three

MICHELLE ANNE
ROLLERCOASTERS

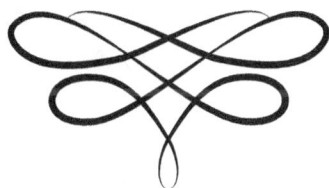

Life is meant for living.

I am Michelle Anne – the older sister of Diane and one-half of *Those2Sisters* – thrill seeker and storyteller. I have a little story for you:

It's a beautiful sunny day at *Movie World* – I feel like the mother of the year... I have secured the annual family tickets – aren't those little buggers pricey? I nearly had to remortgage the house – and have found time in my busy schedule to be the fun Mum and take my girls to the theme park.

My 11-year-old daughter has been begging me to take her on the *Joker* ride for weeks. I later found out it is actually called the *Hyper Coaster*... Looking back, I wish I had Googled it.

We are close to the front of the line and… She chickens out. Foot down, blatantly refuses. No way. Great. The 10-year-old kid next to me grins and tells me he will go on with me.

Now, I am always one to try things once. I mean, seriously… I look around and notice my new ride buddy barely comes up to my armpit and, with a huge grin, tells me it's his sixth time today. It can't be that bad.

I did the *Superman* ride many years ago and figured nothing could be worse than that. The words roll around in my head, *'Well, I can't die. Let's do this.'*

Yep, I wish I Googled it. I might not have been so blasé.

"Ride the longest, tallest and fastest Hyper Coaster in the Southern Hemisphere. Reach speeds of 115kph on this 1.4km track. Experience a menacing 89-degree drop as you descend from the lair of the iconic Joker head from 60 metres off the ground. Thrill Level – Max." (Movie World)

I plummet face down towards the ground – I am pretty sure we've reached the maximum speed of a highway drive in the first 10 seconds. Gravity sucks me with such force out of my seat I feel like I am going to skyrocket into space. I can't even scream. Screaming can only be done when you can function.

Rollercoasters

I shut my eyes and I am pretty sure they are crossed. This makes it worse as I don't see the unexpected turns coming. The next minute, I am upside down (I think). I beg in my head for it to be finished. The straight bit starts and I finally function enough to scream. Surely it must be finished soon.

Nope – I am flung sideways.

Did I mention the thing goes for 1.4 kilometres?! It feels like it is never going to end. I pray and make some promises to God. I will never eat dairy again. I won't drink wine. I will go vegan. Hell, I will do anything.

Make this thing stop!

The man upstairs must have heard. Finally, we are slowing down. I get off – green. I am walking sideways and feel like my head is not attached to my body. My sister and the kids are doubled over in laughter.

Holy shit. NEVER AGAIN.

Why would people do this? Are they crazy? Well – it makes for a good story. Regret is something I never wish to have. It's just like life, really. Crazy, scary, exhilarating and exhausting all at once.

Just like the *Joker* ride, life is up for the taking. I am here to remind you that although scary – life without challenges and scary bits and a thrill level of max is quite frankly boring. *"We all need a few poo-and-spew moments to liven things up."* (quoted by Diane McKendrick herself)

One of those moments includes writing this chapter. I have been procrastinating and making all the excuses. Dragging the chain. I have no idea what I want to tell you all, how I'll get my message across, the pressure to make it as good as my chapter in Volume One. Real, raw and vulnerable.

So, I made a decision. This chapter is going to be told by story. Boring facts are not my thing. That is why Tony Robbins can keep me entertained for 13 hours straight while I am jet-lagged on the other side of the country. He has a huge heart, tells a good story (and is funny as hell!).

So, readers, would you like to join me as I show you that plummeting down towards the ground at 115 kph is all just part of living and that we can use strategies to get through the rollercoaster of life?

Rollercoasters are fun and stories are great, but if they don't have a lesson, then, frankly, I can't see the point. Hopefully, you agree.

Get ready for your lessons!

The Three Pillars

Now, I have a little confession to make. My sister and I have been in business for over five years now and have only just worked out how to explain what we do.

We have spent thousands of dollars on coaches and nobody has been able to illicit what we offer people.

Rollercoasters

They told us we need three pillars.

I told them we didn't.

They told us we needed something tangible to sell.

I told them we didn't.

They told us feelings don't sell.

I swore under my breath and said they do.

Then we went broke.

People don't buy wishy-washy. They want solutions. They want structure.

Nobody knew what the bloody hell we were offering them! Now, here's another funny little story for you...

I met an American guy online. I was lining him up for a potential date. He was good-looking, spiritual and deep. He had a six-pack and a brain! Why not?

What the hell does this have to do with your rollercoaster of life?

Well, he was some marketing guru and gave me these wise words (Cue American accent here):

'People don't buy a quarter-inch drill because they want a quarter-inch drill. People buy a quarter-inch drill because *they want a quarter- inch hole. What exactly are you giving them?'*

Thanks, Chris from America. Turns out, when I Googled it, Chris wasn't as smart as I thought he was, though – this is a very common saying and was first quoted by a German-born economist and professor, Theodore Levitt.

However, Chris was hot and had a six-pack and Theodore was not and had a bald patch, but the lesson was learned! People need structure! They need something to follow and something to grab onto.

I never thought a quarter-inch drill could change my life so much. I still don't know what a quarter-inch drill actually looks like, but it sounds cool and if Chris says it, then it must be true!

Ta-da! The *Divine Hypnotics* module was born. Three pillars that had feeling. It hit me like a lightning bolt during an NLP and hypnosis course. It was so simple – I couldn't believe I hadn't thought of it earlier. I explained the concept to my sister.

She looked at me like I was going mad (I was very excited and talking very quickly). She got that *'Dory'* look in her eyes – the one where she checks out and leaves her body. I persisted. She came back, nodded and said, *'Sounds great.'*

And there it was, the quarter-inch hole was created!

This model really gives a simple way to move through any rollercoaster freakouts we call life.

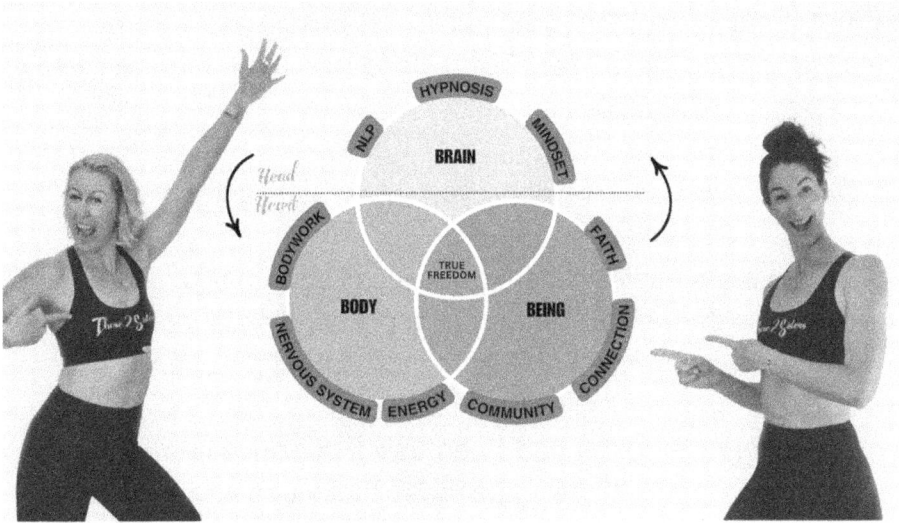

In brief summary:

- Integrate your **HEAD** and your **HEART**.
- **BRAIN** – Rewire your brain.
- **BODY** – Move the feelings through your body.
- **BEING** – Connect with yourself and your community.

Downward Dogs for the Win

'You can't teach an old dog new tricks.'

Oh yes, you can. I am an old dog and over time, have learned MANY new tricks.

It's the low moments when everything has gone to poo – the moments when you think you can't go on, that build the resilience muscle. Resilience is just like a brain; it needs training.

To be clear – no, the brain is NOT a muscle, it's an organ (I have a Science degree) but it does contain lots of nerves that can change over time.

Did you know that 'rewiring your brain' is exactly that?

It is the brain's ability to reorganise itself by forming new neural pathways throughout life and in response to experiences. The saying was wrong – you CAN teach an old dog new tricks.

Without realising it, I had been using our brand new *Divine Hypnotics* model to navigate those tricky ups and downs for many years. I had been rewiring my neural pathways and teaching myself new tricks.

I was a very different person 12 years ago to what I am today.

Picture this:

I'm a boss woman, Sgt in Charge of an extremely busy intelligence office at the *Acacia Ridge Police Station*. I think I'm doing pretty well, smashing out the work, being super organised, multi-tasking like a pro. I am getting all the shit done (the GSD club leader for those of you who have read *Volume 1* of the *Aligned Woman's Way*).

On the surface, I am smiling, but I fail to tell people I am on the edge; I am teetering on burnout; I feel overwhelmed, hyper-stimulated and full of adrenaline. The work list is under control, but I am NOT. I go home to an empty house (before the kids).

Rollercoasters

I lie on my back in the driveway and stare at the clouds. It's all I can do. I am losing my words and my memory and actually wonder if I am experiencing early-onset Alzheimer's.

I am getting shit done, but I am also quietly losing my shit. Seems counterproductive, really.

I think I'm a great boss because I'm doing it all. I have my game face on at work and nobody is any wiser.

Wow, was I proven wrong?

One of my young admin staff went missing from the office. After some investigation, I found out she was having her own meltdown. I asked my Senior Constable where she was. He tells me she is next door at the station talking with the Inspector (the boss nobody likes – every office has one! I will spare you the details).

Why would she go and see HIM? Why didn't she come to see me?

Her answer? *'Oh, you were too busy.'*

Mic drop. I lost it. I had worked so hard. I cared so much, but when she needed me, I was not there.

How had my life come to this? I was stressed, overwhelmed and letting my team down.

I decided to take up hot yoga to calm my mind.

Just like the *Hyper Coaster*, I don't do things by halves, so I signed up for a 30-day hot yoga challenge. 90 minutes of hot yoga every day for 30 days.

Yes, you read that right – yoga in a sauna for 1.5 hours a day every day for a whole month. Clearly, I didn't have kids back then!

Again, I wish I had Googled it. I probably would have chosen the one-minute, 50-second rollercoaster instead – rookie error.

Sweaty or not, I find the challenge working. I am calm, nothing is phasing me, my mind is clear, and I am easily taking on new tasks. I can listen and be present AND get the work done. I feel like a NEW WOMAN. Now I know why.

- **I rewired my BRAIN** – each class was a 90-minute meditation.
- **I moved my BODY** – each class was moving the stress through my body and giving me feel-good hormones.
- **I connected with my BEING** – I was quietening my mind to connect with that thing bigger than myself. I had also found a community.

Downward dogs for the win!

Find Your WAY

Looking back, I realised we had created OUR version of Mind, Body and Spirit. *Those2Sisters* way.

It made complete sense that yoga ticked all the boxes for me. But how do we bring this into everyday life?

Let's get clear here: I am NOT telling you to go out and do yoga every single day for months on end. Although I promise you, it would definitely help – I am still addicted to hot yoga 12 years later. It truly is magical.

What I am suggesting is that if you find yourself in the menacing plummet from the *Joker's* head, you find your way to take back control. If the ground is spinning and you need to shut your eyes, what can you do to steady the ship?

You will know what YOU need. Your Whisper will be telling you (go back and read Volume One if you need some reminders on how to tap into your Whisper)

When it all becomes too much, here are some questions you can ponder:

- How can I connect my head with my heart and bring my brain, body and being together?
- What three steps can I take RIGHT NOW to bring me back to even ground?
- How can I simplify these three steps to remember them easily?

The outside sub-pillars are only suggestions – these are the techniques we use. You may have your own way. We use things like NLP, hypnosis, meditation, somatic bodywork and spiritual practices. You may have your own things in your tool belt.

I had another lightning bolt moment today during our *Coaching Couch* webinar. I asked the participants to come up with their three steps and make an acronym out of them, something that resonated with them and was easy to remember. The results were fantastic – entertaining, clever and on point.

The invitation is now open for YOU to find YOUR acronym that works for YOU.

Make it fun, memorable and meaningful.

Here is mine:

When I am plummeting, I make a sure BET with myself against that nasty *Joker* (he even menaces me from the card deck!). I BET that I will win and that I BET that I will get through this.

B – Breathe (and calm my thoughts)
E – Energise my body (shaking, moving or exercising)
T – Trust and have faith that everything is working out for me

You can steal mine if you like. Or do it your WAY.

What is your acronym? I would love to hear what my creative readers come up with! Send me an email at *michelle@ those2sisters.com* and tell me yours. That would make my day!

Rollercoasters

If you can take back control, you can change the outcome. It's that simple.

When all hell breaks loose and overwhelm rears its ugly head, pull that acronym from your back pocket and flash it like your fake ID at the nightclub! Shhh, I only think I did that once.

In conclusion, I want to leave you with a few reminders.

Rollercoasters can be scary but fun. They make for a good story. Life can also be scary and fun. It also makes for a good story, or two.

Do you choose to:

Sit out on the sideline because you don't want to puke?

or

Do you choose to jump on for the wild ride and make a BET with the *Joker*?

You all have a BRAIN, a BODY and BEING, so use them to your advantage.

An old dog CAN be taught new tricks and it's never too late.

You got this.

Flash that acronym like it's your entry to paradise.

Thrill Level Max is the only way.

ULTIMATE 48 HOUR
A U T H O R

NATASA DENMAN

" Writing your first book is not about the book, but about the
person you become at the other end of it. "

www.writeabook.com.au

Chapter Four

NATASA DENMAN
JOURNEY FROM HONEYMOON TO MASTERY

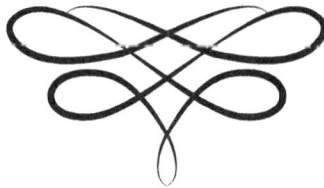

'It's not about writing your first book; it's about the person you become at the other end of it.'
(Natasa Denman)

This is my own quote that I have been sharing for over a decade and back in July 2018, I shared it for the first time with Diane. She had come to my half-day *Ultimate 48 Hour Author* seminar in Brisbane and ended up being the volunteer to have a book unpack done in front of a room of over 40 other aspiring authors.

Many times, she has told me how nervous she was that day, but that little whisper deep inside pushed her to put her hand up and volunteer to be the example in the room. She did a fabulous job playing along with my instructions, and we came up pretty much with what her first book would be then and there: *Rise Up – Your Soulful Guide to Success.*

Weeks later, she attended her *Ultimate 48 Hour Author* retreat in Victoria, once again full of fear and apprehension, so much so that her neck muscles seized up and she could hardly move. My husband Stuart and I coached her through this. She improved but still had more work to do on her fear.

Six years on, I have watched Diane's journey unfold right in front of me, to the point we are collaborating on this book (her fourth) and she has been featured in my latest book, *Book Sales Won't Make You Rich.*

I have witnessed her seasons and cycles in her own personal development, as well as the amazing business she has built to date. I have loved seeing her charge more, host fully booked retreats and bring her sister on board full-time into the business so they can continue to thrive and serve a bigger audience.

The key things I have noticed about Diane that make her unique are her spiritual connection to her intuition and rock-solid discipline in taking action – not perfect action, but progressive action that keeps moving her forward in life and business. I am so happy to now call her a great friend and someone who truly has this ability to listen to people.

Personally, I have seen many seasons and cycles since starting in business 14 years ago. I trust that my chapter can help you with the practical nature of running a business and what to expect along the way.

My goals were always to survive longer than the stats that doomed small businesses. First, it was to be around longer than one year, then three, and then the big one was 10 years. My next goal now is to get to 20.

I find there are three stages that you will experience as a business owner. During those three stages, there are going to be the usual four seasons – summer (when things are booming), autumn (when things slow down), winter (when no one seems to be doing anything), and spring (the ramp-up period to the next boom).

Generally, every year is going to have these four seasons, just like the weather. I used to get frustrated and depressed around autumn and winter cycles, but then I saw it happen over and over, so now I have the wisdom to expect it and learn to ride it out.

I want to spend more time discussing these three stages so that you can recognise where you may be at and how to navigate them.

Stage 1 – Honeymoon

Don't we all love the honeymoon stage? This stage is obvious in relationships and anything new we get excited about. In business, it has been said that an employee has an 'entrepreneurial seizure' and jumps into starting something that they can be in control of so that, ultimately, they have their dream lifestyle and work the hours they want, making decisions as they please.

Yes, this is true. With this new decision and excitement, we tend to have a never-ending supply of energy to take action. Nothing is too hard. We tend to invest in ourselves and our business – sometimes too much – and spread ourselves thin. Any balance around family, social life and intimate relationships tends to go out the window.

You feel like you are working 24/7, but it doesn't bother you. You spend lots of time on promotional activities that cost little or no money but costs a lot of your precious time. You are basically in love with your new venture and want to spend every waking moment with it. It's wonderful, however, not sustainable and it's the toughest stage you must make it through if you are to remain a business owner.

This is where lots of new small businesses fail, in the first 12 months or 1-3 years. They either run out of money due to overinvesting, or time burns them out because 24/7 is not sustainable. I remember my little voice inside saying, *'Is this what life will be like from here on in?'*

Rejection and failed attempts are aplenty, and this is too much for those who don't have the tools to move past it and take the next step. Most business owners dislike sales and marketing, yet this is the key to passing the honeymoon stage and going into routine.

Stage 2 – Routine

If you have made it to the routine stage – congratulations! You actually have a business that can sustain you and your family and hopefully, you can continue to build it up. After all, a business that is business-owner-reliant is still like a prison sentence where if you are not there, everything falls apart.

During this stage of your business, you may start to hire employees to take over particular departments of your business. After all, you should be the best at sales and marketing what you do, so you must be spending most of your time in these departments rather than admin, customer service, or bookkeeping.

You most likely have developed a proven method and are building lots of testimonials that support that. Start writing your systems and passing them on to a virtual assistant or other people you end up hiring. Go slow and steady so that your infrastructure is built firmly and your clients remain raving fans who continue buying from you.

During this stage, you start setting boundaries on how much time you devote to your business activities. You may decide you won't work weekends anymore and have holidays back on your annual schedule. Slowly, you will most likely set up your business to run like a traditional business during normal business hours. That's not to say you won't have busier periods and times you work late and weekends, but this will reduce as your systems and staff will support you.

Be aware: Routine can set in and make things annoyingly repetitive. Unlike during the honeymoon – when everything was new – here, you are pretty set in how things are done and you rinse and repeat. The key is continuing to innovate and improve for the sake of you, your team and your clients. Inventing new value is what will keep you growing.

Stage 3 – Mastery

It has been said that you reach mastery in a particular area after spending 10,000 hours doing that same thing. In business, I feel this is once you pass 10 years of operating in your niche. By this stage, you may become a household name or someone who gets recognised when out in public when you tell people what you do.

You may be regularly spending money on paid advertising so people are seeing your ads and brand over and over. This brand recognition is powerful and finally, your hard work seems to become easier to execute. Potential clients come to you, and you don't need to be chasing as much. Your raving clients send you referrals and hot prospects, and your testimonials speak for themselves.

This doesn't mean you take the foot off the pedal, chill and put your feet up. Your role in your business moves from a sales and marketing pro to a trainer and leader for your team.

You are responsible for ensuring the systems in the business have been fully documented, each department knows what their roles are, and they are doing them well.

Most likely, you will have a sales team in charge of taking calls and closing – they will need most of your attention as they will be the lifeblood of your business. If they don't perform, you will need to step in and save the business.

During mastery, you *must* take care of your people. This is no longer just about you and your clients. Your team is what will either make or break you. When you have an amazing team, you can take holidays and extended periods away from your business, and it will still thrive. I must stress that you have to continue to innovate and problem-solve – the nature of marketing, sales, and your industry will change over time. Keep your finger on the pulse – you are the brains behind your business and that is why you reap the biggest rewards.

Let's get even more practical:

Far too often, I come across businesses and individuals who are confused about the sequence of what and when things need to happen in their business.

As a result, the business never really takes off as time and money are focused on the wrong things. It's like going on your first date and asking the other person, *'Will you marry me?'* and then asking them, *'What's your name?'*

It never ends well, does it?

So here's a rough guide – emphasis on 'rough', your business needs may be very different, so take this with a grain of salt – to what you should focus on depending on your business's financial situation.

STAGE I - Start-Up Phase ($0 - $25K annual turnover)

- Know thyself and know who you are serving (be clear on your ideal client).
- Practise delivering results first.
- Develop the art of asking for referrals.
- Practise doing business without fancy websites or business cards.
- Get clear on what specific problem you are uniquely solving for your clients.
- Practise being okay with asking for money in return for your service.

STAGE II - Growth Phase ($25K - $200K)

- Niche, Niche Niche (Who are your core customers? e.g. injury lawyers in Mornington Peninsula, families with twins, hair salons with organic products, etc.).
- Learn the art of value creation in any situation with your prospects (know their pain points better than them).
- Learn the art of high-value sales with integrity.
- Learn the art of relationship-building.
- Build your email database with your unique products.
- Nurture your leads with compelling offers.
- Connect with leaders/connectors and find out what they need in their business and how you can support them.
- Look for speaking opportunities as much as possible.
- Connect with individuals who run big groups and events to know how you can add value to their groups.

- Invest in microsites (squeeze pages, blogs, giveaways) and small-scale marketing.
- Create a system for delivering your products and services.
- Create scalable processes and product strategy for the next stage.
- Invest in marketing and credibility-building opportunities.
- Learn to sell from webinars/stages/video promos.
- Build your team for your design, marketing and event needs.
- Provide ongoing value via blogs and giveaways.
- A full-scale website can be useful; however, if you have learnt the art of value creation well, you will be full of referral clients who will pay a premium for your services (again, it depends on your specific business needs).

STAGE III - Scalability Phase ($200K - $2M)
- Learn the art of high-value, high-energy sales.
- Work on your own shadows and switch from 'transactional' aspects of your behaviour to 'high value' ways of being.
- Read up on Joint Venture Partnerships.
- Learning to raise price points.
- Add-ons and upsells to existing products.
- Online programs (can be in earlier phases if required).
- Leading by results and testimonials.
- Greater investment in credibility and marketing.
- Powerful promises and requests structure with other players in your industry.
- High-level orchestrated product launches.
- Sharing stages with luminaries in your niche.

- Automated systems in place for marketing and lead gen (can come in earlier stages as well).
- Greater focus on group events and bigger clients.
- Affiliate programmes, franchising, licensing, etc.

STAGE IV - Contribution ($2M+)

- Focus on connecting with other national and world leaders on specific issues at hand.
- Your teams and automated programmes run your business.
- Up your own game at greater JV programmes, speaking engagements, etc.
- The formula remains the same; however, the outcomes become even more personal for many as the focus may shift to contribution and giving back to a greater cause, which, as a result, allows for greater cash flow.

Your Inner World

I know I have talked a lot about practical do's and don'ts, so for the little time I have left with you, I'd like to talk about the importance of spending time working on your inner world. Your mental health and resilient mindset also need to be nurtured on your journey to success and scaling your business through its cycles and stages.

Some of the things I spend time working on for my mindset include:

- Morning 10-minute guided meditation via *YouTube* before I get out of bed to exercise.

- Exercising four times a week makes me happy and energised for the work ahead.
- Reading 10 books a year on mindset/personal development/spirituality.
- Time off – travel four of every 12 months and work smart the other eight.
- Trips away with girlfriends at similar business growth stages as me and sharing our tough times.
- Chatting to my husband, who is my rock and always reassures me that all will be okay and it will work out.
- Getting out of the house if I have been working online too much and getting among people.
- Going somewhere warm – it always makes me happy to escape Melbourne and go to my Gold Coast house.
- Listening to and watching inspirational videos and attending events with awesome speakers.

My quiet inner voice is always guiding me, and I have learnt to trust it more and more as each year passes.

I feel blessed, supported, and loved by everyone around me. I don't know if it's because I have been consistent in working on myself or if it's just me.

If I were to go tomorrow, I know I have made a difference, lived an adventurous life and left behind a legacy I am super proud of.

My wish is for every single one of you reading this to experience that and simply **smash it out!**

SUZANNE READ

" Being an inspirational caring woman for children to look up to is equal to Motherhood! "

www.beyondthewidow.com.au

Chapter Five

SUZANNE READ
MOTHERHOOD

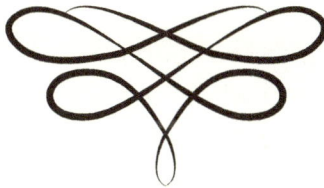

'The state of being a mother' as defined by the Oxford Dictionary.

When do girls decide that they want to be mothers? When they are very young. Through our own mothers, we play with dolls that we call babies. We create make-believe worlds that are two parents and a baby.

Then, we baby that baby for years. We feed that baby, put the baby to bed, bathe the baby, take the baby on walks, and go to tea parties. We do everything a mother would do at such a young age. The baby isn't real, but we are conditioned to be mothers from a very young age.

Then we start to go through our teenage years, and mothering comes back in again. We start to become sexually active, and the first thing most of us do is use methods to prevent motherhood.

Then, you have a long-term partner, and you are conditioned again. But now the conditioning is from everyone around you. And the questions start, *'When are you having children?'* or encouragements like, *'You will make a great mum.'* And the comments keep coming, and you keep saying, *'One day, one day.' 'Not yet, we want to buy a house.' 'Not yet, we need to travel.' 'Not yet, I am focusing on my career.'*

Then, one day, for most women, it just happens. You go off your birth control, and within a few months, maybe a year, maybe through IVF, you conceive the baby that you've always been conditioned to have!

Well, that's when the fairy tale comes true. That's when it all works out in the end. But that's not my story. That's not my fairy-tale ending. I didn't have children; I couldn't conceive a child, and I am writing this chapter to give you a perspective of how it feels to never use your womb for what we were given it for.

Let's go back to the start and recall the story of my journey towards becoming a mother.

I wouldn't say I had a totally normal hormonal cycle when I was a teenager. I was 14 and a half years old when I got my first period. I did ballet, so I was tall and skinny, and the hormones were never stable because of that.

Motherhood

At 16, my mum took me to the doctor because my periods weren't right, and I went on the pill. I needed to regulate my periods because getting your period during lessons while on stage, in leotards, is embarrassing at the highest level for a teenager.

From 1988 to 2008, I was on the pill for 20 years. I did come off it for a short period in 2003, around eight months, because my husband Robert and I decided that after three years of marriage, it was time to start trying. After trying month after month and having no natural success, I went back on the pill and stayed on it for another four years.

I regularly had pap smears throughout this time as I had been sexually active from 17. In 1999, three months before I got married, I had an irregular pap smear result. I had CIN4 cells in my cervix (one step away from cancer) and needed them burnt off to ensure they didn't develop into cervical cancer.

Six weeks after the procedure, I was back to normal. Sexual activity was pain-free and outside of yearly pap smears, which would continue for the next 20 years; I didn't think that this might have caused me to not be able to have children.

None of that changed my thinking about having a family. Robert and I named our children. I always wanted to have a boy first, and he would be named Jonty. Then a girl and her name would be Ashra. Our dream of the perfect family was a regular conversation.

After going off the pill in 2008 and making a commitment to being parents, we started the monthly process of trying when it was right. I bought ovulation kits and made sure I was ovulating as per the instructions. We even did the legs up in the air process to make sure all of Robert's sperm would stay inside and pollinate that little baby of ours.

I would pray and wish for no period the next month. When I was three or four days late, I would do a pregnancy test. We never got a positive result: no pregnancy, no child.

In 2009, we moved to Brisbane for my career; even with the success I was having at work, we continued trying after we moved. I didn't go back on the pill and hoped that nature, in a different location, would take its course and I would fall pregnant.

During the first 10 years of marriage, our friends started to become parents. We became godparents to a number of children, and the kids all loved us. We played with them and spoiled them because we didn't have children of our own.

I recall a day when my oldest goddaughter, who was eight at the time, said to me, *'Auntie Suzanne, I don't want you to have kids because you won't love me as much.'*

At the time, it was so sweet but also wholly gut-wrenching.

At times, when my friends or family would talk about the challenges of parenting, and I would put my own thoughts out there, I would be told, 'You wouldn't understand; *you're not a mum,'* or *'When you're a mum, you will understand.'*

These comments shook me to the core and always made me upset and emotional. They didn't understand how hard it was to be part of a conversation about parenting, much less be put down because you can't be a parent.

We saw a fertility doctor in Brisbane in 2011. We knew we had to get some tests done and find out if there was an issue with our fertility. They did all the tests. Robert was fine, all my internals were fine, there were no blockages, no cysts, just age!

The doctor told me that we were most fertile at the time of our first period, and if I had wanted to be pregnant at 14, I would've conceived. But now that I am 38, my egg count is low, if there was any at all. Conceiving by myself probably won't happen. I will need to think about IVF and come back and see him when I want to take that step.

We left his office with a pile of brochures and a big decision to make. We knew several people who had successful IVF outcomes. I had a best friend who had had a rough time through the 10 years it took her to have two children. But she had two children, a boy and a girl, just like we wanted, but I didn't know if we wanted children enough to go through that.

I don't remember much discussion about it. I left the booklets in the study and looked at them regularly. Time would pass, and we would continue to have intercourse at the right time each month, but nothing was happening.

After trying for three years, with an amazing job and life, we started telling people that we weren't going to have kids. It became easier to say those words than explain what was really going on.

Robert and I were turning 40 in 2012 and 2013 and decided if we both really wanted children after those milestones, we could do IVF then.

In the background, the expectation of having a family also materialised. In 2011, I had a conversation with my mum about her expectations of me having a grandchild for them. I wasn't aware that her own need and want to have grandchildren from her daughter had been a weight on her. My brother's wife was pregnant with his first, I couldn't understand why it had to be me.

I couldn't conceive, and my family never asked me why. Probably because I was saying we don't need to have kids; we have our nieces, nephews, and godchildren to be second parents to. I know now that that was a defence response. The want to have kids was always there, but I had to protect my heart. I had to protect myself, especially when I knew that the reason we couldn't conceive was me.

The doctor had said it. Not prioritising conceiving when we were in our twenties contributed to the outcome. Every woman is different, and conception shouldn't be taken for granted. Maybe the treatment I had for cervical cancer had also had an impact on conception. It was a possibility, but I will never know.

In September 2013, after our amazing 40th birthday trip to Mexico, we were dealt the final parenting blow. Still not being able to conceive, and after a month of the flu for Robert, Robert was diagnosed with an aggressive leukaemia.

Motherhood

Within 24 hours of the diagnosis and being told Robert had to start chemotherapy in the next 48 hours, we had to make the heart-wrenching decision of whether we wanted to freeze Robert's sperm.

I left the decision up to Robert. He had just been diagnosed with leukaemia and was told he was to stay in the hospital for the next month for aggressive treatment. The thoughts that were going around his head of a diagnosis that could take his life and then the need or want to deposit sperm into a cup was not an easy decision.

We sat in the hospital room for an hour, part of it in silence and some talking about what life would look like without children. Then he told me he couldn't. He said even if I wanted him to, he couldn't do it. I took both of his hands and said it was okay. After 14 years of marriage, we are an amazing team. We don't need children to continue to have a great life together. Robert's life was way more important to me than a baby.

Then that was it. The decision was made. We couldn't have children now. The focus was on Robert, and I couldn't even think about children. We were now always going to be the couple with no children. The decision was now out of our hands; the chemotherapy was more important.

For the next six years, proceeding Robert's diagnosis and then his death, having children wasn't part of my conversations anymore. No one asked us after the initial conversation of telling people that we made the decision not to freeze Robert's sperm. I continued to love the children we had around us.

We spent time with them, and I gave them the parental love that was inside of me.

Without realising it, I had decided that talking about children while Robert was sick wasn't worth thinking about or grieving over. I had other priorities, and I rarely thought about motherhood or the loss of motherhood.

That was until Mother's Day 2020, 11 months after Robert died. During the peak of COVID-19 in Australia, when the country was locked down, I was living by myself on 35 acres with no one to visit me, no children to celebrate me being their mum!

Yep, the realisation of not being a mum to another human hit with full force. A few friends sent me messages saying, *'Happy Fur Baby Mother's Day'*, but at the time, that just rubbed salt into the wound. The wound was starting to fester and open beyond my thinking as every hour and minute passed on that day.

I grabbed my puppy and rocked back and forth on my bed. The grieving of never being able to have children had begun. This loss, on top of Robert, had now surfaced, and there was no way of stopping the deluge of tears. Tears that I deserved to shed, tears that I didn't think would even appear because I hadn't had the opportunity to be a mother.

I walked out to the ridge in my back paddock, and I screamed, cried and hugged that dog of mine so hard that even he started to whimper and cry. The decision that had been made, which I knew was the right decision at the time, was having a huge emotional impact on me now.

Motherhood

I deserved to cry, I deserved to grieve, I deserved to feel lonely, to feel angry at all the mothers who got the choice that I didn't. I didn't want to celebrate this day; I didn't deserve to celebrate this day. Why see all the happy faces on my socials, celebrating the gift of life, when it hadn't been given to me?

Like I always did that day, I pulled myself together for my mum and sister-in-law. We video-called each other for dinner. I sat by myself in my house, with my dog, celebrating my mum. I had put my big girl's pants on to be unselfish and grateful for what I had around me. The love of a mum, from a mum who had supported me through so much. For a woman, that meant so much to me. Geez, does the grief of not being a mum ever stop?!

Not yet... There was another hurdle I still had to go through.

In 2022, I attended my first women's retreat. At a luncheon, I met Diane McKendrick. We had both written books through the same publishing company. Mine was *From Wife to Widow*, hers was *Millionaire Mum*. For the first time that year, I was free on the weekend that *Those2Sisters* had their retreat.

A lot of the emotion that I experienced in the first couple of days at the retreat was related to Robert's death. The grieving process, the dissolving of guilt, shame and judgement, was being released. On the third day, we did a womb-healing meditation that sent me through the next grieving event.

As we lay down, the soft meditation being spoken, circulating in my head, my instant reaction was, *'Why am I here? Why am I doing this? My womb doesn't need healing. It hasn't even been used for what we are born to use it for. I don't need this; this is ridiculous; get me out of here; I don't belong here.'*

Then, 45 minutes into the meditation, I left. I got up and left the mediation, left the room, and went back to my room. And I started purging. The toxic thoughts, the want to be a mother, started coming out of all of me. Through this, I was not even recognising it was about the loss of motherhood!

After 30 minutes, I came back to the room – the room of mothers who were discussing their experiences and tenderly holding their wombs or each other in comfort during such a beautiful experience.

Then, the next purge happened: They all looked at me. Diane asked, *'How did that feel for you, Suzanne?'*

I started to push back at first, *'Nothing. I don't need to heal something that hasn't been used.'*

Then, one lady said something that hit a core. Hit the spot that made me realise that my choice of being a mother had been taken away from me. My womb missed out on one of the most sacred experiences, and I didn't get that choice.

Then the tears started, and the words of anger, sadness, and grief came pouring out. This is what I needed to do; this is why I was here. This retreat was another opportunity to grieve motherhood to release the pain of not being a mum.

The beautiful thing about being with these women was that they cared. They listened. Their care and kind words, such beautiful love, enabled me to fully grieve the loss of a title, a role, and something that every woman contemplates and most women receive.

After the retreat, I spoke to my grief counsellor about the loss of motherhood. She worked with me over several sessions to process the grief, the pain, the sadness, and all of the emotions that I had pushed down for so long. I cried a lot during that time, although she also gave me an insight that I hadn't had the opportunity to fully embrace.

Like the ladies at the retreat, she reminded me that I had just met an amazing man. This man who I was falling in love with had three daughters and a granddaughter that I could embrace. Whether it was forever or just a short time, they could give me the opportunity to be the mother I never was.

This story has a beautiful ending. I went on to marry that man. James has given me the opportunity, through his daughters and grandchildren, to be able to love, care for and tend to them the way I would've if they had been born from me.

In return, they love me, ask me to guide them, create memories with them, trust and respect me, and say that I am the mother they wished they had had.

I love them as if they are my own.

A wise woman once told me, *'Mothers come in all shapes and sizes, with different titles, but the love from someone who represents themselves as a mother can never be questioned.'*

I believe that now.

Through the roller coaster of life, the challenging times of not being able to birth my own child, and the lessons I was taught through my godchildren, nieces, and nephews all got me to this point in time – the moment in my life where I have become the mum I wanted to be to the children who want me to be their mum!

I know that not everyone who wants to be a mum or has lost a child will ever get over the pain and sadness of not experiencing motherhood to its fullest extent. My experience of loss, the work I have done to love myself, to be proud of who I am, to follow my dreams, and to open myself up to love again, have given me this opportunity.

An opportunity I never thought I would ever get and one I will never take for granted!

NICOLE LADYNSKI

" It's never too late to build your wealth. Educate, Protect, Grow - Diversify "

Nicole Ladynski   nicoletladynski

Chapter Six

NICOLE LADYNSKI

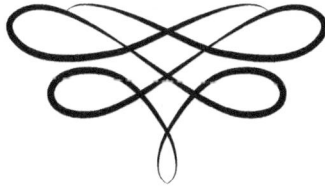

Throughout our lives, we go through seasons and cycles. This is no different when it comes to your wealth.

I personally have gone through the seasons and cycles of starting as a businesswoman with no money, then creating quite a bit of money to then losing it all and creating wealth again. I went completely full circle. The lessons I have learnt along the way has put me in the position I am today. Loving life, living on my own terms and supporting my family, travel and motocross lifestyle.

Two years ago, I met Diane at an online event; she was a guest speaker. Listening to Diane speak, I could feel her energy. Diane and my eyes locked; in that moment, my thoughts were, I need to find out more about what Diane offers; I need to work with her; I had a good feeling. I remember an exercise that Diane requested us all to complete on the call, it was to find out our *Aligned Woman's Archetype.* Completing the Typeform, my results were sent instantly: *'You are an Aligned Woman.'*

Two weeks later, I joined the *Aligned Woman Academy* online course, which is how my *Those2Sisters* journey began. During the AWA course, I learnt about seasons and cycles in my life. When I dug deeper, I realised that this was relevant to my business and my wealth.

In 2003, Nathan (my husband) and I bought our first business in Central Queensland with no money. Crunching the numbers, I saw the potential and went for it.

Being in business was an eye-opener, especially at 20 years old. Not only was I working full-time, but I became a CFO overnight. I had never done anything like this before. The key to starting a new business is asking for help. This goes for anything we do in life. If you're not sure, ask; you will never know if you don't.

I knew time wasn't on my side. I needed to learn quickly and asking for help is exactly what I did. I reached out to people I knew who could guide me, who had the knowledge, and who could give me the tools I needed. I learnt quickly about payroll, record keeping, invoicing, and profit and loss.

Between 2003 and 2009, our business took off; it more than doubled in size, creating a substantial amount of wealth. Life was good on that front. I paid off my mortgage in two years, paid cash for absolutely everything, cars, motorbikes, etc., and set up structures and systems to create more wealth.

On the flip side, the other side of the coin, remember there is always two sides to a coin which means two sides to everything. This is how everything is balanced out. I learned this from Diane and Michelle when I first started my journey with them.

There were many dark days of fatigue, frustration, stress and doubt. Employees not showing up for work, becoming unreliable and I couldn't go on holidays without staff phoning with problems; this even happened on our honeymoon, covering claims and tax bills every quarter. The two biggest problems were staff turnover and tax bills.

In 2009, I was made redundant from my full-time position before becoming a Mum to my beautiful boy. This added a new dynamic to running a very successful business. Sleepless nights and big days are not a good mix. Some days felt like dèjà vu. Actually, for the next two years, we were riding the hamster wheel. Our business hit its peak, and there was no room for growth.

The biggest lesson in business is work-life balance. Watching Nathan go to work to run the day-to-day operations of our business was painful. Leaving early in the morning and returning home late in the evening meant he rarely saw our little boy.

Working six days a week took its toll on all of us. Our little boy missed his Dad and Nathan missed his son. Nathan missed all of our little boys' milestones, which broke his heart and mine. These moments are so special. Then, add on all the stress of running a very successful business.

I grew up with my parents working every day, money was tight and we were always looked after by family members. This is something that I didn't wish for as a parent. Our boy was growing up so quickly.

We had a successful business and an abundance of money, but one thing was missing: connection. Family connection was a huge disconnect. Father and son, husband and wife bond, no amount of money can buy this.

In 2011, I welcomed my second son into the world. A couple of months passed, and my CFO hat was in full swing when a thought came to the forefront of my mind: Let's sell the business and house, buy a caravan and travel Australia for 12 months. This is a way to jump off the hamster wheel and connect as a family.

My Whisper was telling me: *'What's the point of creating all this wealth if you're not enjoying life?'*

No holidays, no quality family time, no fun. I have one life and have been working hard for the past eight years; it's time to start living.

When I voiced my thoughts to Nathan, he thought I was joking at first. I reassured him that I was completely serious. He was so excited and our travel plans began.

Nicole Ladynski

Within five months, the business and house sold and a new way of life began, travelling Australia. It was absolutely incredible, so many wonderful experiences, seeing the most amazing places. Every day was an adventure.

Here in Australia, we are sure blessed with magnificent wonders of the world. We completed a full lap of Australia, including Tasmania, in 12 months.

Leaving my previous life, family and friends behind wasn't even a second thought to me. Living each day, in the moment, having an absolute blast with complete freedom. Imagine waking up each day, no alarm, nowhere to be specifically, no managing staff, no payroll, no nuisance calls, no tax bills. How much lighter do you feel, saying that? This is how I felt.

In the 12 months of travelling, I was fitter, healthier and happier. It didn't just impact me. I could see the difference in my family. Nathan loved being present with the boys, being an active Dad and the boys loved having both of us beside them every day.

To give you a little bit of a perspective, my eldest boy was two years old, and my youngest six months when we started travelling. Some may think *'You're nuts'* but at the time, my intuition told me that this is what my body needed. I am truly grateful and blessed that Nathan was on the same page as me because travelling bought my family closer together, a bond that I will never forget.

After finishing our lap at the end of 2012, it was time to start thinking about what's next. I asked myself, *'What do I desire?'*

95

A couple of things came to me. One, I had no desire to live back in Central Queensland. While travelling, I had a big realisation that my family were no longer serving me. And two, I loved being out in the country, away from people living right next door, out among nature in the wide-open spaces. A new season and cycle was now in seed.

2013-2014 were two big years. As they say, *'Everything comes in threes.'*

New property, new business, new house. For the next nine years, 82 acres west of Toowoomba was home.

Building a new home was different this time; living in a caravan taught me that the little things in life mean so much more than material items. My new home, smaller than our first, had a real country charm; it was beautiful.

My new business allowed me to be at home with the boys and Nathan completed the day-to-day operations. It was completely different from my first business. It suited our lifestyle. Nathan started at 4am and finished by lunchtime, five days a week. Which was great; we were all together every afternoon and weekend. We had a real work-life balance.

In 2016, both my boys were now at primary school. My business was smaller, which meant my workload was reduced significantly. I became lost and bored with no one at home. I decided to find a job during school hours. I accepted a position working for a local optometrist.

The next four years, I went from working part-time to full-time. My lifestyle changed during this time; my two boys decided motocross was their sport. There is a lot of costs associated with motocross, licences, bikes, gear, safety equipment, plus bike maintenance.

With my business and working full-time, I had the finances covered, life was great. Our weekends were full of quality family time and motocross racing between Toowoomba, Warwick, and Goondiwindi.

In 2020, my life changed dramatically, as did most. The pandemic hit hard, businesses were closing left, right and centre, which impacted our business immensely. Nathan's days were reduced by half and my full-time hours also reduced – impacting our income significantly. My boys were now being home-schooled, which they loved because it meant more bike time for them.

Over the next two years, everything started to fall apart. My business never recovered from the pandemic; no matter what I tried, nothing worked. I was pushing shit uphill. Slowly but surely, I watched the business go from profit to loss. I was devasted. I felt so guilty; I am the CFO; how did I let this happen? I should have seen this coming. In reality, this was not the case; how could I see the pandemic coming?

Everything crumbled around me: I was miserable, I was burnt out, my marriage was falling apart, my health was deteriorating, I was now living week to week trying to support my family on my wage only, and the business was in the red big time. I was trying to stay strong, but the stress of it all got the better of me.

I needed to reach out and ask for help. This is where my personal development journey started.

Once I started working on myself and utilising the tools I was given, I began to see everything differently. Reading personal development books on my lunch breaks, my mindset was shifting. My eyes were open more than ever.

I learnt a valuable lesson early on. The five people you spend the most time with, you become. This blew my mind and slapped me in the face at the same time. I was becoming the people I worked with. I also completed another valuable task, *'What are your top core values?'*

Mine: family, health and wealth.

This was my light bulb moment. My life didn't demonstrate my core values. This is my responsibility and something I could change.

Looking at this on a deeper level, realising that nothing changes if nothing changes. It was time for me to sit with my thoughts and ask myself once again, *'What do I desire?'*

My answers were pretty straightforward, so I didn't need much time to process them. I desired my loving relationship with my husband, to be present with my boys – I missed them terribly – to be free again and to travel, this time incorporating the boys' love of motocross.

My current life didn't represent this at all. For all my desires to come to fruition, I needed to do one thing. Walk away from this season and start again. I have done this before and I can do it all again.

Walking away from my business that was now worth nothing, quit my full-time job that was no longer serving me, selling my house/acreage that I absolutely loved and taking the boys out of mainstream school. Walking away from a business isn't easy but when your back's against the wall, you have no other option.

I said to myself, *'This is happening for me, not to me. I am removing everything that isn't serving me and allowing more space for new opportunities.'*

This is a very powerful exercise.

As one door closes, another door opens. My beloved house sold within three days in 2022, receiving a higher-than-expected price. The biggest task was packing up the house and preparing to travel full-time following the motocross circuit, with no end date in sight.

What do you do with all the material items you collect over the years?

You don't realise how much you collect until it's time to move. Deciding not to pay for storage fees, there was only one option. I implemented a valuable exercise I learnt in everyday life and thought I would give it a go in this situation. I was blown away with the results.

For every item, I asked myself, *'Is this serving me?'*

WOW, so powerful. Before long, I had next to no items. Everything I kept could fit either in the caravan or truck. My biggest takeaway from this exercise is realising that moments are more important than materialistic items.

In 2023, I focused on my health, my relationships and myself. My personal growth journey intensified with Diane and Michelle. As I travelled with my family, racing motocross every weekend plus training during the week, I started an online business. My heart was full but something was still missing.

Vision and purpose. I had an idea but it lacked energy and belief. It felt like someone else's vision not mine. I needed to go deeper. With Diane's help I got clear, I now had direction. My podcast series was born – *Life, Love, Motherhood after Trauma*. I had people say to me this isn't a good idea. It broke my heart, as this provided a space to have a voice and share my story.

I struggled in my online business; I was people-pleasing, it felt icky, I was kicked down by people around me, I felt not good enough, and I spent so much time on the computer with no reward. I was pushing shit uphill again; this time, I was in denial. I realised I was totally out of alignment. Again, I asked myself questions, this time, *'Why does it have to be this hard?'*

I had been working with Diane and Michelle for quite some time, and one of the important lessons I had learnt is alignment. My mind was telling me one thing and my body felt the complete opposite. What I was doing wasn't working because it didn't align with me or my values.

Nicole Ladynski

Attending *The Renew Retreat* with *Those2Sisters* in October 2023, I had a massive breakthrough, released a lot and walked away lighter and with a higher vibration. Not long after the retreat, I asked the Universe to show me a way that I could create wealth to fund travelling, the boy's motocross and something I could do without sacrificing family time. I desire to be around like-minded people who have the same values as me.

Two weeks later, a new opportunity presented itself to me and it ticked all my boxes. Better still, I could see past just travel and motocross. For the first time ever, I was clear on my vision and purpose. The two things I lacked, I could now see clearly as sitting on a boat, out at sea, on a bright sunny day, looking through the crystal-clear water. This was the beginning of something big; I could feel it through my whole body.

In 2024, I attended two retreats with *Those2Sisters*. I felt a huge release at the *Energetics of Life* retreat in March. This retreat changed my life; the brick I had been carrying with me my whole life was now gone.

Diane and Michelle's work is absolutely incredible; words don't do it justice; it's something you feel deep within.

If you haven't attended one, I highly recommend that you do. Each retreat is different, but you receive exactly what you need. Diane and Michelle know how to hold space, bring all the beautiful ladies together and come away with new connections, new tools, and a new version of themselves.

My new business is educating others in diversification. Throughout my businesses since the age of 20, a couple of key factors have been missing: one, education and two, diversification. My very first business created a substantial amount of income, but I wasn't educated on what to do with the wealth; I just stored it in the bank. If I had known how to diversify at a young age, it may have just saved me some heartache. It's never too late to start.

At the *Energetics of Business* retreat in June, my highlight was standing up in front of all the other beautiful business women sharing my business. It felt amazing, I could feel my energy and my passion beaming out of me like rays of sunshine.

I am passionate about creating wealth, education and diversification. Wealth creation doesn't need to be hard. Money flows when you are in *Alignment*, your body and mind are open and you are ready to receive.

I'm creating a substantial amount of wealth again, but this time, it's different. It's fulfilling my vision and my purpose in life, and I am having a lot of fun along the way with my family and my communities.

This is Alignment.

I am blessed and truly grateful to be surrounded by like-minded souls in both my communities, *Those2Sisters* and my diversification family.

Nicole Ladynski

I am in a new season and cycle, loving life on purpose, and my vision is at the forefront. This wouldn't be possible if I hadn't gone through every season and cycle. My puzzle pieces of family, health, lifestyle and wealth appeared in each season and cycle but never truly came together in unison until now.

I am an *Aligned Woman*!

My final message to you as you go through your seasons and cycles is to embrace, learn and grow.

Love and Happiness,
Nicole Ladynski

DR. MARISSA CAUDILL

" Success is not just about making money; it's about making a difference. "

Chapter Seven

DR. MARISSA CAUDILL

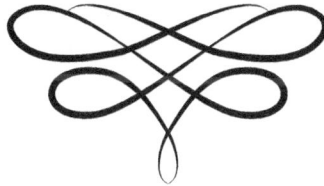

I was introduced to Diane by a series of fortunate events in December 2023 while attending *Date with Destiny*, a six-day event hosted by Tony Robbins in Fort Lauderdale, Florida. There were over 2,000 people in attendance from all over the world. While leaving the bathroom on day one, I saw a woman wearing a black T-shirt with 'SISTER' written in big white letters on the back. I have a younger sister named Chelsey, whom I adore. In fact, Chelsey is such a source of joy in my life that just seeing the word 'SISTER' makes my heart leap. I wanted to run up to this stranger in the bathroom, grab her by the arm and ask, *'Do you have a sister? I have a sister too!'* but I thought that would probably make me seem like a big weirdo, so I restrained myself.

At the end of the first day, we were all assigned buddies. Diane got assigned to Catalina Matiz[1]. Catalina and I had hit it off and exchanged info while waiting in line to enter the event, so this was synchronicity #1.

On day three of the event, I had written that one of my top four goals for 2024 was to travel to Australia with our kids. My husband, who was at the same event but seated on the opposite side of the room from me, had written the same goal of 'travel to Australia with the kids' on his 2024 goals list. This was not planned. We had mentioned it once, maybe, as something that might be fun *someday*. This was synchronicity #2.

I finally met Diane during a break on day four. She was sitting with Catalina at the back of the convention centre, and we began chatting. Within 10 minutes, I had learned that she and her sister run retreats for women in Australia. She handed me her card, and I saw photos of them in their black T-shirts with 'SISTER' on the back.

She told me the next retreat was scheduled for March 2024, just a few days before my kids' spring holiday. She had two seats left. Upon hearing this, my husband and I locked eyes and nodded, understanding that this was synchronicity #3.

---

[1] Southern California physician, Mum, businesswoman and co-author of the first iteration of *Aligned Woman's Way*.

With just a few clicks on my phone. I booked two tickets to the *Energetics of Life* retreat with Diane, planning to attend with my sister and have a family vacation afterwards with my husband and kids.

While it turned out that travelling with my sister, kids and husband wasn't possible in March 2024, my best friend of 27 years was able to attend with me. Diliana is my soul sister, and we had an amazing time. I can't even put into words what those few days meant to us.

I came with an open heart but no expectations. I was blown away by how talented Diane and Michelle are at creating a safe and inviting space that allows women to bravely expose their souls to strangers and connect with their most deeply aligned purpose.

But, let's back up. I need to tell you a bit about me so you can decide if this chapter is one that resonates with you. Marissa Caudill, MD, PhD, is a type-A personality. Goodie-goodie, straight-A student. Teacher's pet. First born child. Leader. Rule follower.

Like Michelle Anne, I have been a card-toting member of the 'Get Shit Done' club my whole life. I am NOT good at relaxing; that is for lazy people! Words like *energy, vibration, manifestation* and *soul* used to make me roll my eyes because those aren't things you can measure, test or see, so clearly, they are woo-woo and ridiculous.

Well, that is who I was. Happily, I have undergone a transformation over the last two to three years. A transformation that has opened my heart and exponentially increased my energy and passion for life and my work. Like when a bird jumps off a cliff and soars, held up by the invisible force of air, I now know that I can fly in my life and reach limitless heights.

Spirit/source energy/God – call it what you want. There is an invisible force and energy that is responsible for our conscious awareness. That energy is everywhere, all around us. It is infinite, not bound by time. It is there when we're awake, when we're asleep, and when we're in deep sleep.

When we are born, our consciousness arises from it, and it is what we will return to when our bodies die. Our true selves are part of that energy. My answer to *'Who are you?'* is not my name, the mind coming up with these words, the body typing them, my titles, or my relationships. I am simply loving energy. Knowing this now, I'm full of faith, joy, and awe and just enjoying the amazing ride that is life.

I've been asked to write about seasons and cycles in life and business. Just calling myself a businesswoman feels a bit weird, to be honest. As Di would say, *'It's not yet hardwired'* in my nervous system to think of myself as one. I am, however, fully aware that I'm travelling through seasons and cycles.

Two and half years ago, after buying three rental properties, I quit my high-paying clinical job as a child psychiatrist. I now manage four properties in four states, am a general partner in a multimillion-dollar real estate syndication, and I am building a kick-ass business (*The Parent Doctor*, you can check it out at www.theparentdoctor.com) that will have a greater impact on kids' mental health and parent-child relationships than a busy clinical career as a child psychiatrist ever could have had.

I'm able to do all this while being present for my kids, being in the best shape of my life, sleeping eight hours a night, having time for travel and friends, spending summers in New Hampshire and the school year in Los Angeles and having a marriage that gets better and more loving every day.

For me, the key to making this happen was allowing a metamorphosis to happen. I shed my old identity by having faith that a bigger, more beautiful identity awaited me. You know how a caterpillar forms a chrysalis, digests its body with enzymes and emerges as a totally different creature? My journey feels like that.

Sidebar: Did you know the dormant cells in a caterpillar's body that become the butterfly are called 'imaginal discs'? Each disc contains the genetic information to form a specific part of the adult butterfly. Isn't that amazing? What do your imaginal discs have in store for you? If you sit with yourself, your body will tell you.

My caterpillar self is a medical doctor; a psychiatrist. My training was long. I've always had a need to prove that I can exceed expectations and do it all, and then some, which I now realise stems from what Diane calls my 'Wounding' but has nothing to do with my 'Whisper'.

My Wounding told me I needed to be the biggest, fattest, best caterpillar and THEN I would be safe and could live and die contented. As a result of choosing this high professional mountain to climb, I was 35 years old before I completed my training and got my first 'real job'. Because 14 years of post-college education topped by two medical board certifications must be a recipe for a winning caterpillar, right?!

As a double-board certified MD based in an urban area like Los Angeles, I had great earning potential as soon as I finished training. On the surface, I had it all – a great job, a hard-working, dedicated and loving husband (David, also an MD/PhD psychiatrist whom I met in training), healthy kids, high earnings, excellent benefits, hired help in the form of a housekeeper and nanny, lovely house, nice friends. So, why was I irritated and exhausted all the time?

It took me a LONG time to figure this out. I blamed my husband for YEARS and our marriage suffered. I thought if only he would help me more, I wouldn't have so much on my plate and I would be less overwhelmed and happier. I thought that if he really loved me, he would just *know* this, and I wouldn't have to tell him or ask him for help. All of that was a story I told myself. None of it was true.

I was, and am, responsible for my own happiness.

As are you.

As are we all.

But this is not what most people accept as true. Instead, we easily find camaraderie in blaming others; we use the language of victimhood. Life happens *to us*. This view externalises our power and fuels a sense of helplessness. This became my identity, and I was not alone.

I had a big, loving community of unhappy women I surrounded myself with. We were all awesome. So, if we were all going through similar stressors, the problem was clearly not *us*, right? It was *them* (meaning partners, bosses, husbands, in-laws, kids, societal pressure, the patriarchy).

Many coffee dates, social media posts, and girls' nights out were spent connecting with others on this low-energy plane. We were unhappy caterpillars, envious of the rare butterflies we encountered, with no idea how to become one and no knowledge that such a transformation was even possible.

I now wish I could go back and tell myself that my true self knew the answer I was seeking and that my body would have known the answer instantly if I had known how to tap into what I needed at that time, but I didn't know.

From 2007-2013, I was laser-focused on achieving my primary human needs – significance and certainty – by completing my education with residency and fellowship. And secondarily, love and connection, by getting married in 2010. With those things achieved and needs met, I thought I would finally feel safe and content. I was waiting to feel 'whole' by reaching some level of professional mastery and union with a good man. I yearned to be higher. I was climbing and climbing, but I was on the ground.

Then, we had our first child in 2012, a son. Welcoming my child was amazing; my life instantly changed. The love I felt was all consuming; he became my top priority. This felt wonderful, but in the years that followed, I again felt incomplete and off-balance. I figured it was because I was learning how to balance work and being a mum.

From 2012 to 2018, I was seeking an answer for what was missing in the wrong places (different ways to work and earn, hiring more help, decorating the house, more 'self-care', more stuff), but I didn't realise that.

We welcomed a second child in 2016, a daughter. I thought, *'Ah, now I will feel complete,'* but... I didn't. I had grown into a bigger, fatter caterpillar on higher ground. I was safe, but I was not content. I didn't feel high enough, but I had come to the top of my mountain.

Again, I thought it was just the adjustment to new motherhood and that it would pass. Things were more complicated, so I rose to the challenge. People advised me to *'outsource, stick to your zone of genius, track your time, meal prep, schedule time to get a massage and plan date nights.'*

So, my type-A brain made spreadsheets:

- To try to work out my ideal work schedule;
- To plan the kids' schedule;
- To plan the nanny's schedule;
- To come up with meal plans;
- To commit to when I would work out;
- To block off when we would take vacations;
- To schedule date nights.

But I still didn't feel content or at peace. Despite feeling overwhelmed, I felt full of unused potential energy and exploding with a desire to test my limits. Driven by financial goals (I still thought the answer was more money) but also a subconscious belief that maybe I wasn't working hard enough to earn my butterfly wings, I took a full-time position as a child psychiatrist with Kaiser Permanente in 2018. The pay was great; the sign-on bonus was huge. Only the best, most efficient doctors succeeded in this place.

I saw two to four new patients daily, 10-14 total patient visits daily, five days a week. This should do it, right? I was going to earn some wings.

But my inner caterpillar kept whispering. It was like the one in *Alice in Wonderland*, nagging me by asking *'Who are you?'* over and over. I didn't have time to listen or answer; I was too busy earning my wings. I tuned it out.

Then, the pandemic hit. Truly, it's a blur in my memory. My older child, in first grade, sat in the dining room eight hours a day on *Zoom*. He was miserable. I was working from home, seeing 13 patients a day via *Zoom* at a folding table in my bedroom. My daughter was young enough that she seemed okay and just happy to be home. My husband was working from home, too; I would hear him yelling at his hard-of-hearing elderly patients from the office to explain how to turn on their cameras so they could have a video visit.

Every day seemed the same for many months, and it wasn't good. The slowed pace of everything made the Whisper grow louder, *'Who are you?'* It kept me up at night.

The good thing about dissatisfaction is that it can drive you to act. In late 2020, I took a course in real estate investing (again, with a goal of making more money, because if I couldn't grow wings, maybe I could buy them?) and created a compelling future that would be my why.

I wanted to have *Camp Chelsey*, a home in New Hampshire where we could take our kids in the summer. I grew up in New Hampshire and my sister still lives there with her husband and kids. My dream was that we would be able to enjoy summers together with all the cousins hanging out and that my sister and I would get to spend time together, since she's a teacher and has summers off. I didn't know it at the time, but this was my first conscious experience manifesting a desire.

In June 2021, my sister sent me a *Facebook* message posted by one of her neighbours who wanted to sell his home off-market. By July 2021, we were under contract and closed on the house in September 2021. My soul was singing. I knew we were going to do this, no matter what it took. Summer 2022 was going to be amazing.

I had my first breakthrough in realising that I could make empowering choices to live in alignment and on purpose in November 2021. I had attended my first Tony Robbins event, a four-day whirlwind called *Unleash the Power Within* – it's amazing, if you ever get the chance to go, do it!

I had no idea what I was getting into. I thought it was a business seminar and it was not that at all! I came home a *'new woman',* according to my husband. I realised that I had been creating my misery through my thoughts and choices and default emotions and that I held the power to change them. I was a psychiatrist and I didn't know this! This led us to have what David calls the *'best year of our marriage'* following November 2021.

By spring 2022, I had to talk with my boss about our desire to spend summers out of state. Almost all of my patient care was still being done virtually, so I was planning on keeping my job and working remotely. Unexpectedly, she came back and told me that partner physicians had to be in California, so I handed in my resignation.

I'm greatly simplifying these events for the sake of this chapter, but this decision was gut-wrenching. By this time, I had worked in this busy clinic for over four years and had over 1,800 patients under my care. I had been a practicing psychiatrist for 15 years. It was my identity.

I worked closely with two other child psychiatrists serving hundreds of thousands of patients in our catchment area. We couldn't meet the patient demand as it was. If I quit, I knew I would be putting overworked, burned-out physicians, therapists and nurses in a position to be even more burned out. I felt a lot of guilt about that. Then, on top of that, the waiting list for kids to see a child psychiatrist was over three months long. The demand was huge in 2022 because child mental health, which had already been on a negative trend for years, was acutely suffering from the strains of the pandemic.

My departure would make patients suffer with further delayed care. But my whisper was now incessant, *'Who are you?'* The pain of continuing to do something that wasn't aligned for me was greater than the pain of my guilt, so I gave three months' notice. My last day as a caterpillar was May 31, 2022.

I then took the first summer off I had taken in 30 years. I highly recommend that everyone take a summer off – at least once every 30 years. It was amazing. I contracted COVID-19 in May 2022 and recovered, but I was so tired throughout June.

I took three to four-hour naps daily and slept nine hours at night. I can't know if that was from COVID-19 or if my body was just finally allowing itself to recuperate after years of pushing my limits. Either way, this was the first stage of forming my chrysalis – rest and recuperation.

Wounding provides a very strong impetus for our behaviour and it shapes our caterpillar identity. Whether it's physical, sexual, or psychological trauma or just our internalised sense of how we 'should' be that arises from our family of origin and early life that form our ego-driven sense of self, wounding raises cortisol levels and gives us energy to unconsciously drive us.

When we are out of alignment, our Wounding fuels us in this way. This can lead to great accomplishment, but it comes at a cost. Poor sleep, increased appetite, sweet cravings, alcohol or drug use, abdominal obesity, depression, irritability, low energy, trouble concentrating.

All of these can be symptoms of sympathetic nervous system overdrive (a.k.a. Wounding). I had them all, though I didn't admit it to myself. It was hard to see this as abnormal when all the other big-shot caterpillars I surrounded myself with had the same problems.

Since entering the chrysalis phase of life, however, I have come to see that any butterfly existence is better than even the best caterpillar existence. Listening to the whisper is winning.

I quit a job that paid me over $370k per year, with bonuses, benefits and a pension. I was good at it. I was, in theory, in a helping role as a physician. I liked and respected my co-workers, but I knew I wasn't really helping my patients to the best of my ability in that setting.

For me to make the greatest contribution I can, to fly *above* the mountain top, I had to go outside my comfort zone. I've had to accept a lot less certainty and enzymatically dissolve my life as I knew it. My imaginal discs are still encoding my transformation as *The Parent Doctor* butterfly, but I know that the genetic programming that's needed is all there.

Currently, I'm programming my nervous system, with Diane's help, to feel what I know is true. That I can have enough and seek more.

I am enough. I have enough.

I was a big, fat caterpillar on a high mountain. It is precisely because I am enough and have enough, that I could take the risk I'm taking in this chrysalis. I can give more, be more and create more as a butterfly.

The 'more' comes from first being enough; you have to be enough to be able to give and create. Creating more and having more and receiving more are NOT in conflict with having enough, they arise from having enough. You inspire others when you successfully program yourself to know that you are enough.

What really matters in life? What really matters is laying it all out. Making yourself uncomfortable by growing your reach and impact to have the biggest possible positive influence on others.

Spread love in the ways only you can.

This is different for each of us, of course, because each of us is a unique soul manifestation of source energy.

My butterfly self will do work that is fulfilling and that gives me flexibility. It will mean that I am no longer trading hours of work for dollars at a 1:1 ratio, even if it's a high ratio.

In fact, especially when that ratio is high, it becomes binding and restricts your connection to source energy and your purpose.

I know there are many big, fat, tired caterpillars out there living in safety on high hills, earning lots of dollars, but they are missing out on so much. Are you one of them?

DR. RUPINDER SHARMA

" Hold the vision and trust the process. **"**

www.drrupindersharma.com

Chapter Eight

DR. RUPINDER SHARMA

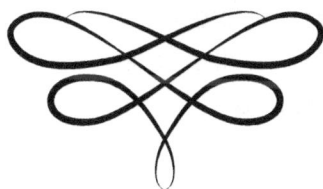

Sitting back to reflect on my career and life as a mother, wife and chiropractor, I can recognise my growth and alignment of coming into my own.

A kaleidoscope comes to mind. Looking through the glass and twisting the tube, the shapes and colours align to form a beautiful pattern with every twist. This is how I see my life: an ever-changing pattern in the kaleidoscope of life.

As women, we move through seasons and cycles, from our monthly cycles to the seasons of life. I acknowledge that as I've moved through the seasons of life from Mum of babies and toddlers to now teenagers, my practice and business have evolved along with these seasons.

A little about me. I've always been an outlier, a go-getter, a woman who knows what she wants and if it wasn't happening for me, I'd do everything in my power to make it happen. I did this quietly and shyly, in my own way, without all the fanfare. It wasn't always that I trusted the process or that the next step would appear. That has come with experience and wisdom.

I was born and raised in Canada with very strict Indian parents. I went away to university, where I found my first taste of freedom and then to New York for chiropractic college. That was my first big 'outlier' step. Chiropractor, what even is that!? Is that even a real doctor!? Oh, the questions I got.

That didn't bother me as much as a comment from a chiropractor I went to shadow. He was a man in his 40s, and I was a young, naive university student trying to figure out what I wanted to do with my life. As I stood watching him help his patients, he commented that I should consider another profession because it would be too hard because I'm small and I'm a female.

Now it's comments like that that usually light a fire under my butt and make me want to prove otherwise. And I did just that. Off I went to New York for another four years to complete my Doctorate of Chiropractic.

I've been practising for 20 years, from the time of publishing this book. I've always had mentors and coaches who have positively influenced and encouraged me. Every single time the student (me) was ready, the teacher would appear.

In this season of my career, I closely look at the balance of feminine and masculine energy when it comes to my business and career. From the moment I graduated, my mentors and coaches have primarily been men; throughout my career, I've had only two female coaches.

Chiropractic is by far a very masculine-dominated profession. I thought it may have been that I needed more structure and foundational steps to make it in practice and that was why I was drawn to male coaches. So my coaching sessions would consist of lots of numbers and this is how you do it and this is the script and these are the steps, with little room to wiggle. And I accepted that this is how it must be done. What do I know?!

It wasn't until six years ago that I really honed into my feminine energy and, I guess, accepted my femininity and realised I didn't need more masculine energy. In a male-dominated profession and business, male energy dominates decisions and employees and runs a numbers-oriented business. I needed more softness in my life. I needed a place where I could just ebb and flow with my feminine energy.

When I realised this, my practice started to shift for the better. I felt into what I needed to do for myself. What really pushed me along, if I'm completely honest, is when my mum passed away three years ago. That deeply affected me.

With the grief, sadness, anger and whirlwind of emotions, I tried to make sense of them, which you never can. I found a way to let those feelings guide me. Again, my practice shifted. There was a part of me that questioned whether I made the right decision. I didn't do my pro/con list; instead, I reflected on what I needed and trusted.

There was an era of toddlers and building a practice. This energy was scattered, to say the least, as we juggled between day-care and bringing my three-year-old to work with me; as he coloured and read in the corner, I adjusted my clients.

Thinking back to those days, my current clients remind me of those days 10 years later. That was a season for push. Everything was a push, from getting enough sleep to trying to juggle and thinking it was all working. I could laugh out loud now! Ha!

Then came the young children era; both kids were now in school, and I decided to embark on my business. I decided to open a practice in a little town called Boonah. Not knowing how to run a business and hire staff, I figured it out with my husband's support. At this point, I still had male coaches. The practice grew so quickly that I had to open more days and hire more staff. It was a quick learning curve. During school holidays, my boys would come with me to work and sit in the spare room with their iPads and books.

My practice grew as I grew. Literally, as I worked on myself, not just learning and growing in terms of chiropractic techniques, etc., but as a woman, as I did the inner work, my practice grew. I knew that my superpower was to inspire and guide women to health and self-awareness.

Dr. Rupinder Sharma

Chiropractic allows me to help and connect with women at a deeper level. Not only do I get to lay my hands on to help heal, but I get to make heart-to-heart connections with these people. I create a space to allow them to be vulnerable and feel safe as I guide them to self-awareness.

I dove deeper as I learned more about myself and wanted to know more about myself. I did a neuro-emotional technique seminar where I learned how to release and neutralise emotions in the body that could be playing a role in disease in the body.

This gave me another avenue to go deeper with women. Chiropractic is one of those professions where people come in with all sorts of preconceived notions of what it is and how it will work. I absolutely love opening them up to a new way of knowing their body and having that emotional awareness. I absolutely love watching people literally blossom under care.

Five years into my business, I became a life coach to help women understand themselves. I know there is so much we can understand about ourselves; just when you think you know, there's another layer.

Feminine energy is meant to flow, be vulnerable and be wild; we are like water, filling a vessel. It is powerful energy when harnessed and used for good. What this world doesn't provide for us is the safe vessels to be vulnerable and to be able to flow.

Women like Diane and Michelle have done an amazing job creating environments where we can safely harness our femininity.

As I move towards my mid-40s, again, my practice has shifted, and as a result, my family and I thrive. Two years ago, I decided to open a practice from home because driving to Boonah was becoming a chore. So, in my manifestation journal, I wrote down exactly the type of chiropractor I wanted to work alongside in my practice. When he arrived, I was able to take a step back and open up from home.

Not knowing how it was going to work, I told my husband he wasn't going to have his TV room. He was fine with that :) and we made it work. I absolutely love working from home, the ease with my clients and most of all, the ease for my family.

When people step inside my home or in my practice in Boonah, they comment on the energy they feel. To me, I couldn't receive a bigger compliment. I take pride in what I can create for my clients and how I can help them.

As I settle into this cycle of life, let's see what stirs up inside next.

The key to this is to listen to your soul, heart and spirit. We need to quieten down the background noise and lean into what our hearts are saying. It doesn't always make sense and it may not be a sequence of steps, but that is the beauty of our femininity.

When we get too structured into the running of a business, how it needs to be done and what should happen next because that's how it's always been done, we can easily drown out those Whispers, as Diane calls them. We live in a very masculine world, where things are according to certain times, etc. The beauty of today's world is also that we can design our lives however we want.

When I started my business in Boonah, I started at 9:30 and finished at 4:30, with a 1.5-hour lunch in between. The comments I received from both men and women felt snarky, *'Isn't that nice?'* to which I would smile and nod. It is!

I designed my practice around my family – when I needed to drop them off, pick them up and rest for myself. And now, with my home office, my intention is the same. I'm able to drop my kids off at school and I can look after myself as well. And it is nice – it's really nice – unapologetically nice!

With my 40s comes a certain knowing, but I hear that knowing grows exponentially in your 50s.

As with everything, we move through different seasons; rather than rushing through them and waiting for the next, it's important to reflect. This has definitely given me a huge opportunity to reflect on the season's past.

An unconscious belief that I held was that women didn't know how to do anything correctly and weren't as successful as men. When this came to my awareness, it was a massive shock to my system, with a heavy side of denial. How could this be me, Rupinder, the feminist, and this is a belief I hold? But maybe reflecting on this now, maybe I feel so strongly about women and had such an overt reaction to that chiropractor in my uni days, because I knew I had something to prove to myself.

Well, I worked so hard and fast to clear that from my nervous system! I made a list of all the women I looked up to in my life, mentors on TV, in the movies and in books and in my life. This was a huge shift in me.

These deep realisations of doing the inner work make the biggest shifts in our lives and can change the course of our lives.

I know what I bring to the table and what I have to offer the world as a woman, as a chiropractor and as a life coach. It may seem like I have my shit together; I hear this often from those looking from outside in and there is nothing that makes me cringe more. I promise I don't have it together. I wish I did. What you see is a woman trying to navigate this world with her family, bringing her gifts to the world to help more people and trying to have fun while doing it!

Chiropractic is a healing modality that focuses on the body's ability to heal itself. Everything you need is within you. Many times, we look for external validation, but the answers are always there. Chiropractic care focuses on your nervous system's ability to heal. My job as a chiropractor is to remove nerve interference, and your body does the rest.

Having a clear intention of seeing the person before they are healed and whole sometimes means holding a bigger vision for them that they can't even see yet. And if they hang in there for long enough, they begin to see the possibilities for themselves. This is the beauty of chiropractic with intention.

Dr. Rupinder Sharma

My practice has moved from seeing lots of babies and toddlers to pregnant women, families and now to middle-aged women and helping them navigate mental and emotional awareness. As our needs and awareness shifts, everything around us does as well.

COVID was a testing time as the career I had built was on the line, as it was with many. Decisions had to be made that I had to live with. During this time, my mum passed away.

Being from Canada, there was a two-week hotel quarantine on the way there and on the way back. So the decision was made that I wouldn't go, rather stay at home in Australia, with my husband and kids, rather than grieve by myself in a sterile hotel room for two weeks before I could see my dad and my brothers and mum.

It was a sad time. It was confusing; it was anger-filled. The world went from being an oyster to light years apart. I couldn't make sense of the fact that I wasn't there for my mum's funeral; I couldn't be there with my family. I couldn't be there with my brothers to grieve. It was a very difficult time.

Again, my practice shifted. As my bandwidth changed to what I was able to hold for myself and those around me, there was a shift. I learned to slow down. I found myself and still ask myself, what would Mum do? Or what would she say in this situation?

My mum gave me an amazing template to work off of and gave me an incredible opportunity to grow in leaps. I knew she wanted more for me than what she was able to do, which is why she always encouraged.

When I wanted to go away to university and chiropractic college, it was with encouragement. Then, I wanted to move oceans away for the experience; again, it was with encouragement and pride. My mum was a risk taker, a *'Let's give it a go, what's the worst that can happen?'* kind of woman. If she was afraid or worried, she never put it on me; it was only a *'Go try.'*

It's in this season that I wish I could have more time with her now. Being in my 40s, I remember my mum when she was this age. She had the world on her shoulders and me, a typical bratty, know-it-all teenager.

To you, I say, never feel guilty about rest.

Organise your life around how you want your life, not how others think you should.

Unapologetically, rest and play.

Let go of the guilt.

Lean in.

Do things with the right intention.

I think it comes with age and experience that as we learn to feel into things, we innately know what will be next. As we learn to trust those feelings, they will not lead us astray but, in fact, bring us into our power and knowing.

This world is designed to not feel but do. We need to do the opposite.

Dr. Rupinder Sharma

The 20s were the illusion that I had it together, the 30s was the hustle and now, the 40s is the leaning in.

I'm not sure whether that is how the seasons and cycles go or if I was always to lean in. It's through life experience and personal growth that I've settled into my skin.

It's taken me 44 years; I hope it takes the next young woman a lot less time. My hope is for those reading this to lean in, listen to their hearts, give themselves time, drop the hustle and watch themselves blossom.

I love the life I've created. I can sit back and be very proud of what I have accomplished in terms of my career and business and family. There is always a give and take; nothing is ever 100% balance 50/50, especially when you've got kids and a family.

In our early years, we move through life on others' terms: do this, do that, no, not like this, like that, as if you're like me, you didn't question it; you just did because that was going to lead you to the pot of gold at the end. Then, somewhere along the line, you start to see incongruence and you start questioning, then the doubt sets in because others are questioning your decisions and eventually, you plant your feet firmly on the ground and claim what's yours and move forward.

I wish every woman on this planet could claim what is theirs.

A mentor of mine in the early years often said to me, *'When you know your why, the hows take care of themselves.'* When you know why you are doing something or why you want it, the rest works out.

I love this gift of chiropractic and the ability to connect that I have been given, to work with all kinds of people who trust me to help them to better health and awareness.

I guard it as a sacred gift and thank you to every person who allows me to place my hands on them to help.

JO KNOTT

" The beauty of tomorrow lies in todays growth. "

Chapter Nine

JO KNOTT
IN THE JOURNEY LIES THE ANSWERS

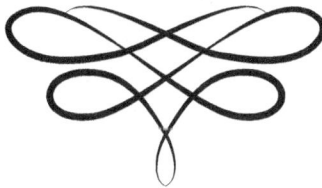

Co-authoring this book has been the start of a life-altering and significant cycle in my life and business. I am profoundly proud to be contributing to this book, even though the process has made me doubt myself incessantly.

I wanted to write about becoming the owner of a 'successful' multimillion-dollar business, but I've struggled with imposter syndrome as my business doesn't entirely fit the criteria I have put around it. That being, a successful multimilliondollar business that affords me the freedom to be home (more hours than at work) with my two little girls, Florence (4) and Scarlett (3), the monetary freedom to travel and explore the country with my family, share in business success with my husband – raising each other up and cheering each other on, to gift generously to family and friends and leave a prosperous legacy for my kids, while I retire early and pursue other ventures to fill my cup. All of this while coming from a place of peace, mindfulness and alignment with myself.

When I first put words down for this chapter, I really didn't believe I could write about being aligned and successful. I felt like such a fraud. Then I started writing. I did the thing that I didn't think I could. This was an absolute metaphor for my entire journey in life and business. And now I get to share the journey that led me to owning MJK, having the experience to operate it, but also the seasons and cycles that have contributed to my limiting beliefs, self-doubt and imposter syndrome. All the things that have held me back from amplifying and claiming the success of my business and life.

I am Jocia (pronounced Joe-sia) Knott. I became Jo at age 11 when my primary school teacher in New Zealand couldn't pronounce my name, so she preferred Jo to Jocia. Talk about an identity shift at a young age. I grew to love Jo. It was easy to say and easy for others to remember, which became crucial for a young migrant girl trying to fit in and find her place in the world.

I am a South African-born, proud Australian with a portion of my heart carved out for New Zealand. The Tri-Nations in one soul.

In the Journey Lies the Answers

I am the proud 50% share owner of MJK Industries (MJK) (with my husband), a business that provides engineering, fabrication, and installation services for structural, mechanical, and piping projects in the manufacturing and processing industries, among other industries.

I grew up barefoot in South Africa, snacking on fresh fruit and raw veggies after school in my parents' fresh produce roadside stall. When I wasn't snacking, I was serving customers – a seven-year-old counting out change to round out the total amount the customer had given me. I would stay up in the evenings helping to count the cash revenue, deducting staff wages and expenses to then determine the profit made for the day.

For a safer, better life, my parents sold their worldly possessions, said goodbye to family and friends, and bought one-way tickets to New Zealand. I struggled to find my place in this new country and school. The class was fraught with controversy over claims that South Africa had poisoned The All Blacks in the 1995 World Cup. The Kiwis are intensely passionate rugby union supporters, and I found myself ostracised over something I knew little about and was not in control of. The connection with my identity, culture and ancestry began to fray as I attempted every which way to detach myself from this controversial act. My desire for connection and acceptance overshadowed my sense of identity and innocence at just age nine!

It's interesting that author Brene Brown shares her research across the globe, identifying two fundamental human needs: connection and belonging. Yet you can't achieve these without vulnerability and the release of shame – ironically, the two things I resisted for many years and still, at times, do.

At the beginning of my teenage years, I joined the high school rowing team. The mateship, comradery, support, and relationships I experienced in those years were unmatched. I found my place, a place where I felt connected and accepted. At home, I was celebrated for being good at this sport. It was common to be told that no dream or desire was out of reach: *'There is nothing that can't be learnt or mastered to enable you to succeed.'*

When we lost races or my training wasn't at its best, I felt a sense of deficiency, defeat, and shame. I had no tools or guidance to lead me through the feelings of shame for losing. I believed that by admitting shame, I would also be admitting weakness. I sat in the narrative of *'Anyone can be good if they try, except for you because you are trying and you're not good.'* This narrative would shift later in life to *'Even if you are good, anyone can be just as good as you,'* diminishing any uniqueness or exceptional qualities in my work, personality or life.

At age 15, while dodging shame and vulnerability, my dad graduated as a chiropractor, and the family once more migrated to a (slightly less) foreign country so that he could take up private practice in a small industrial town in Central Queensland, Australia. I still had no tools to support vulnerability and shame; my default was to bury vulnerability for fear of judgement.

On weekends and after school, I worked in the chiropractic clinic. I always had a smile fixed on my face as I greeted patients with politeness and professionalism. I always received compliments on my personality; I liked that. It sure beat vulnerability and shame. And so, people-pleasing became my default.

I witnessed that business success comes with sacrifice of personal time, fulfilment, healthy relationships and the growth of personal and emotional intelligence.

By the time I transitioned from school age into my early 20s and started studying Law at university, I was pretty good at people pleasing; I placed big bricks on any intuition bubbling up and replaced any vulnerability with an outwardly confident nature, a complete mask for my self-sabotaging.

I continued in legal practice with a somewhat arrogant confidence, fuelled by a fear of vulnerability and judgement. I lived by the concept that I should know everything I ought to know about legal practice because I had graduated. I battled with asking for support or guidance in areas where I wasn't confident (most things) for fear of criticism for having completed my degree yet not knowing how to navigate practical elements.

Thankfully, regardless of how many stacks of bricks I'd piled onto my intuition over the years, intuition prevailed. I recall the first time I really followed my intuition. I was sitting with the legal practice manager after submitting my request to travel back home over an extended weekend to see my Ouma Ann, knowing it would likely be the last time I would see her (and it was). I was unequivocally told, *'Jo, there comes a time when you will have to choose – your career or your family.'*

I knew what I was choosing.

As the universe would have it, this resignation resulted in me securing a new role in legal practice back home, and meeting Matt, my now-husband.

Over the 2010 Christmas, Matt and I had been gifted flights to South Africa for a family holiday and reunion. I was yet again faced with a rejected annual leave request; my intuition once again rose to the surface and I knew there wouldn't be a choice in the matter of going or not. This trip was one of the greatest gifts I could have gifted myself by way of listening to my Whisper. My uncle, Machiel, whom Matt and I had formed a special bond with while in SA, passed away in a car accident just six months after our visit.

In early 2011, I discovered a noticeable lump in my right breast, the size of a 20c piece. I gave up on the GP and headed straight to *The Wesley Breast Clinic* in Brisbane. They are renowned for their model of care. I don't recall being nervous or anxious about the process. The staff were incredibly supportive, informative and optimistic. I met with Dr. Letitia Hanson, who has remained my overseeing physician to this day, to discuss the ultrasound results.

The scan revealed a cyst-like formation. I recall the words so well – they changed my life and perception of acceptable risk from that day forward:

*'We're fairly confident that this is just a benign cyst, but there's a **1%** chance of it being something more sinister, so we'd like to do a biopsy just to be sure.'*

In the Journey Lies the Answers

It was late in the afternoon when the biopsy was done. I recall it hurting like hell and left a whopping bruise on my right breast.

The results phone call came the next morning. It was Letitia, in her sweet and loving voice, *'They've picked up just a little something, Ductal Carcinoma In-Situ (DCIS). It will likely need to be removed. I'll organise for you to see Professor Owen Ung,'* who was an endocrine and breast surgeon.

My mind was reeling.

Time slowed. The following day, I met my beautiful lifelong friend Clair in Brisbane, and she held my hand as the journey unfolded.

Matt was working away, but he called to listen in on the consult with Prof Ung, hearing the words drop: *'Your mammogram shows the DCIS as widespread, throughout 75% of your breast. The best course of action is to remove your breast entirely – a mastectomy. I can refer you to a plastic surgeon who can perform a reconstruction at the same time.'*

I was 24 and absolutely devastated!

As the words left Prof Ung's mouth, I heard Matt say, *'I'm going to jump off the phone now and sort some flights; I'll see you in the morning.'*

This man stood by my side like I could never have imagined possible, and I knew from that moment that we would be together forever.

We took the next few weeks slowly – nipple-sparing mastectomy and reconstruction that nearly didn't work, seven days in the hospital, nail-biting lymph node test results and decisions around future treatments, genetic testing and recovery. I settled, knowing I had done all I could to protect myself, and I would walk through life as a breast cancer survivor.

I was forced to slow down during this time of my life, and with the gift of time and Matt's financial support, I was blessed with the chance to pivot my career, which accelerated me towards owning my own business and taught me the majority of the industry skills I use today. Without breast cancer, these opportunities would not have existed. The universe has divine ways of intertwining all our interactions to shape us into who we are.

I was completely oblivious to the vast world of health and safety in the workplace, especially in an industrial setting, until Matt became victim to unsafe work practices, having had a 30kg tool bag narrowly missing him as it fell from a scaffold above. I threw myself into studying workplace health and safety. I had no clue about the industry or the practical nature of health and safety, but I knew how to apply the law – both pragmatically and fundamentally. This became my greatest asset. In times like these, I didn't doubt that I was able, just my ability to be great. My confidence mask pushed me to keep going.

I continued to work in health and safety for years. I enjoyed learning and being in a significant role where I could interact with people from all walks of life, influencing mindsets through my persona and inquisitive nature.

But the industry is ruthless, masculine, resistant to change – and far more political than pragmatic. My confidence and assertion were broken down, and the layer below was self-doubting, delicate and self-sabotaging. I came face to face with many dominant men, their condescending nature spinning me into a frenzy of self-doubt. I needed to keep the tough exterior shell firmly in place as I truly believed this was the only way to survive. I didn't know myself anymore. I actively started seeking answers; I wanted more alignment in myself, in my emotions and in my abilities to be the inwardly confident me that I aspired to be. I innately believed I wasn't broken and didn't need medication to fix me, but I wasn't sure how else I would get there.

I met people along the way who planted little seeds of wisdom in my mind, sparking some confidence in me and nudging me toward exploring self-awareness, emotional intelligence and vulnerability.

Matt and I married in 2016, and only four months after our wedding, and not even three months after declaring and celebrating five years in remission and free of recurring breast cancer, I found a small lump on my right upper chest wall. This time, the diagnosis was a little more ominous – localised invasive breast cancer.

A journey of surgery, tests, embryo sparing IVF and daily radiation for six weeks, followed by three months of chemotherapy ensued.

As shitty as the breast cancer journeys were, I cannot help but be grateful for the opportunities it created. It truly changed the trajectory of our lives.

Before we were married, Matt and I had furnished the idea of owning our own business and as a result, MJK Industries was born. During my chemo and radiation downtime, I tinkered with the setup of MJK. I had never set up a business but I figured it out without even realising that it was a culmination of all my life skills sown together that enabled me to take action and believe in my power.

I did everything from scratch, using *Snip* to design the foundations of our logo, word to develop our business cards, spreadsheets to track projects, creation of estimate and quote documents, invoicing direct from *Xero*, and the set-up of IT, software, shared folders, etc. Much of what I knew came from my inquisitive nature in my role in health and safety.

I've never been very good at sticking to my lane, even before any business-owning concepts were alive. I wanted to know how projects were run and how payroll was managed. I contributed to tender developments, subcontractor evaluations, administration support, and contract negotiations, and I even dabbled in procurement. Admittedly, all these aspects held relevance to health and safety. I am a very holistic practitioner and business owner. Every action has an equal and opposite reaction. Without really understanding and accepting that, as a business owner, you can bind your team up in a muddle, create excessive workflows for yourself and your business and you cannot truly understand the outcomes for your clients.

In the Journey Lies the Answers

It has taken me putting pen to paper to write this book for me to realise just how damn amazing I am for having figured it all out, and all the while navigating limiting beliefs, imposter syndrome and immense procrastination over one million things because I simply doubted my ability, didn't know where to start, felt I didn't have the answers and I wasn't able to be vulnerable enough to ask for help.

Having been raised under the umbrella that I could know just as much as a professional, I found it incredibly difficult to seek expert advice, for shame would creep in, often asking… *'Why do you need an expert? You should know these things.'*

I would spend hours, days, weeks, and honestly, even months trying to figure out how to do things (in business and life), burning not only my time (which I now accept as equating to money) but also digging myself deeper into the pits of not being good enough because I wasn't 'good' at doing the things that experts could do with ease.

Returning to health and safety after my breast cancer treatment and recovery, I was on edge with an overactive adrenal system, experiencing anxiety frequently, and I would dread waking in the mornings. I worked stupid hours in the name of sacrifice.

By late 2019, I had resigned from my health and safety role after falling pregnant with Florence. MJK was taking up more and more of my time outside work hours. Even with a newborn, my sleep and 100% presence with Flo were sacrificed for the sake of MJK's success.

When COVID hit, the world and business we had fought so hard to establish and maintain was literally about to crumble with one breath. I can still feel my palms sweating as I typed personal letters to all our permanent employees to notify them that MJK would be closing its doors. A major project that was due to commence was now stalled, with no forecast on when or if it would go ahead. Our advance sales forecast crashed to nothing, and our cash reserves were soaked up.

We woke to the news that our business was deemed essential work. With frantic phone calls to clients and suppliers alike, we were able to continue working on key packages of work that were critical to our clients' business operations. It kept our doors open and our business alive!

In the subsequent months, we picked up enough work to force us out of the small workshop and office space we had been in. I cringed signing the new lease; the cost was four times what we were paying per annum, we had just employed two new staff members and had a five-month-old. It felt like a huge leap of faith.

Only a few months later, we fell pregnant with our second daughter, Scarlett. We were overjoyed, but the work didn't slow down. The challenges grew, with navigating new staff on-boarding, staff performances, increased sales demands and another new premises – with two little ones under two. I don't remember it feeling as chaotic in the moment as what it does looking back on it. I know I lived on anxiety and adrenaline and tried to cram just as much work in with two little ones at home as I did with just one. It definitely didn't work. Scarlett claimed much more of my attention than Flo used to, which I think was probably contributed to because I was giving Scarlett less time than I gave to Flo. The walls started closing in on me. The sleep deprivation, the dynamics of caring for a toddler plus a baby, the marital strains of working together, and both having very strong and often opposite views on business issues, growth and financial considerations were overwhelming.

I was triggered by everything, losing my temper at the drop of a hat. I felt, at times, like I was in a large black pit. I could see the light, but I couldn't get my footing to climb out. With every little step towards the light, I would slip down again and it was starting to feel hopeless. At times, I really didn't want to do it anymore because it felt as if I could never be the mum, the wife, the business owner, the friend or the human I really wanted to be. I didn't want to sacrifice my health, the relationships with my children and my husband for business.

I tried the obvious – putting the girls in care, then more days, we hired more staff to pick up the work that I was covering across the business, but the marital strain remained, and my patience didn't return. I found myself always prioritising work over self-care and my family. I subconsciously believed if I continued to sacrifice, everything would fall into place. But it wasn't; it was just getting worse.

I'd seen psychologists in the past and tried again for a while. Nothing was really shifting, and my intuition pushed me away from prescribed medication, something I felt would merely mask my troubles. I clued on that my moods were significantly impacted by my menstrual cycle, but even so, there was something deeper. I didn't like who I was as a person, I was aware that my Woundings and life experiences contributed to my behaviours, and I simply didn't like it.

Self-discovery, growth and healing of wounds really is a journey. For me, this journey has been long and slow until some things finally started to click more recently. Every little nudge along the road has provided me with tools, vocabulary, curiosity and eventually, the vulnerability to be able to ask others and myself more questions, to tap into my intuition, to hear what my body is telling me and to begin to understand myself – accept the parts of me that I don't like and celebrate the natures I love about myself and I want more of.

I took a leap and started working with Di and Michelle, attending their *Energetics of Business Retreat* and *Inner Love Retreat* and partaking in *The Aligned Woman's Academy*. This leap tied together all the work I had been doing over the years without feeling as if anything changed, and a huge shift transpired.

Through this work, a door has been opened into my soul. I have uncovered the roots to why my limiting beliefs were here in the first place, how those beliefs impact my day-to-day behaviours, including procrastination, frustration and avoidance, and how to transmute fears surrounding these behaviours.

MJK, as it is today, may not be in one, five or 30 years from now, and no matter the outcomes – good, bad or ugly – such as the seasons and cycles of sunflower growth, my personal and entrepreneurial roots are already established in the soil, grounding deeper and stronger with every lived experience.

I have never felt so certain about anything in my life. I feel liberated for being gifted with this knowledge. This power!

AESTHETIC
COACH

ATTRACT | NURTURE | CONVERT

NICOLE
MONTGOMERY

" True self-love isn't about fitting into a mould but embracing every unique trait that makes you, *you*. It's in recognizing that our perceived imperfections are what set us apart, and in cherishing them, we find our true strength. Invest in yourself, not to change who you are, but to celebrate the originality that only you can bring to the world. You deserve to feel your best every day, not because of how you look, but because of the love you have for who you are. "

www.aestheticalchemist.com.au | www.aestheticcoach.com.au

Chapter Ten

NICOLE MONTGOMERY

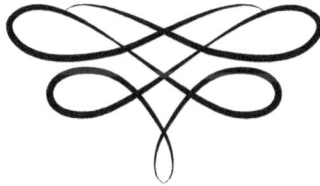

Hello, my name is Nicole Montgomery, a mother of four children and a registered nurse of 15+ years – and I love to help people. Some would say I am a people-pleaser, but I truly feel most fulfilled when serving others. I am currently the founder of three businesses and have one failed business under my belt.

Aesthetic Alchemist is a platform for consumers looking for education, tips and advice within the aesthetic industry. We educate our audience through not only the website but also through our social media channels.

The second business is *Aesthetic Coach*; I am an event and marketing strategist and I help medical-based businesses reach their audience in a meaningful way. Finally, I am a practising registered nurse. I believe in pro-ageing and self-love and find nothing more rewarding than being a part of a patient's transformative journey.

Winding back to 2016, I started *Trusted Surgeons* after seeing how many lives were being destroyed by the lack of regulation and accessibility to cosmetic surgery. As a nurse, I felt powerless and heartbroken seeing patients' lives destroyed post-elective surgery. I wanted to raise awareness and promote qualified surgeons to ultimately prevent patients from suffering the devastating effects of botched surgery.

I saw first-hand patients become commodities, walking advertisements for surgeons, flaunted and sexualised on social media as part of advertising campaigns to attract new patients. There were no independent advocacy services for patients; the industry was confusing for consumers, and tensions among practitioners and surgeons were high.

I have had to deal with cyberbullies from the body shaming movement, which was soul-destroying. I was attacked for *'promoting surgery'* when all I wanted to do was educate. I had to learn not to take everything so personally. I was also called many names as a whistle-blower, which broke me for a while.

I spoke at a government hearing and had multiple senators asking me questions for over two hours. I poured my heart out, sharing patient stories which horrified them. I have had to teach myself mindfulness and actively incorporate positive thinking strategies.

As part of everything I do, I practice self-reflection and if I am not constructive, I easily fall into a negative mindset (which I often do). I've even had a cyber impersonator who destroyed the business *Trusted Surgeons*. Every time I posted anything, the impersonator would pop up on the fake account.

Despite all my efforts, the only way to stop the account was for me to stop posting. I heard a voice in my head saying, *'What the hell are you doing? Why did you open your big mouth?'*

As a result, I went into hiding and returned to work a normal 9-5 role.

A valuable lesson I have learnt is to take nothing for granted; I poured my life into *Trusted Surgeons* over five years and quit within five minutes. In hindsight (years later), I am proud of the work I did and all I achieved. The large organisations started *Instagram* accounts and started educating consumers. The laws have since been amended and I would like to believe consumers are safer.

Rewinding to the early '90s, I was 15 with E-cup breasts and was an average, slim build size 8 and 160cm tall. I frequently attracted the unwanted attention of older men and became accustomed to ridicule. I was judged by men and women; I was frequently called names and I could no longer participate in activities I loved.

I studied classical ballet from a young age. I was the opposite of the ideal ballerina's body, I was long, lanky and had huge breasts. I could no longer wear the leotards and costumes I once adored. My normal physical developmental changes seemed to happen overnight.

One day, I was shaving a few hairs under my arms; the next, I was getting fitted for a huge grandma bra titled the *'Cross Your Heart Bra'* in what was once *Grace Bros*.

I clearly recall going to an event with friends in which we all wore matching tank tops. Considering that my waist was very small and my stomach was flat, I had no issue with my midriff exposed. However, when I appeared in the kitchen ready to go, my dad exclaimed, *'Nicole, you look like a Jersey cow!'*

I was so upset; I was embarrassed and truly ashamed of my body. I wanted to cut off my own breasts. I, of course, was then the only person in my group wearing a huge, oversized t-shirt. I started wearing baggy clothes two to four times too big. I always had huge, painful bra straps to hide.

I was so ashamed and so lonely; I removed myself from friends, I stopped activities, I had nothing to live for and I hated myself. So much so that I wanted to die. This is extremely dramatic, but as I will continue to reiterate, I was 15.

Popularity was important to me; being successful and performing was my life. I had overcome a broken leg and I had physio before school, I practised all the time and still succeeded in passing my RAD ballet exam. I was determined to be a dancer; it was my entire life.

Nicole Montgomery

After the Christmas concert at the *Sydney Opera House*, I realised I no longer could enjoy dancing. I was picked to do a solo, which was 35 seconds of pure excitement for me. Yet, in rehearsal, my breast practically busted out of my shoestring leotard. I had two ballet teachers; one was male and I was devastated.

This was the final straw of humiliation.

When the summer holidays came to an end, I could not bring myself to return to my performing arts school I truly lived and breathed; how could I go back? What was the point? How could I disappoint my parents, who had worked so hard for so many years to pay for my tuition, private lessons and costumes?

I decided I wanted to die.

I went to our medicine cabinet and took every tablet I could find. I took so much I could no longer swallow and I lay crying, hoping it was enough. I recall calling my dad and telling him I had made a terrible mistake. I slurred my words and told him, *'I tried to kill myself. Please come home.'*

The next I remember was in an ambulance. A day or two after in the hospital, the nurse asked, *'Can I bring your mum in?'*

I said, *'No.'*

I refused to see my mum because I was ashamed, I was embarrassed and I did not want to disappoint her. It took a lot of work between the hospital, community support and a psychologist to help me get home. All I asked was not to go back to my school and to not do dancing as I could not endure the shame and embarrassment of my breasts and failure.

I felt I had failed; my body had failed me and I now had no control. It turned out the one person who refused to give up on me was my mum. She insisted I did have control and where there is a will, there is a way. So, we set off to the GP. I was not sure why or what the GP was going to do about my breast size, but Mum had a plan.

The GP thought my mum was crazy, I was awkward and uncomfortable, and the entire process was humiliating. Thankfully, my mother is persistent, and we got our referral. Knowing I had to go through this process again with a plastic surgeon was something that weighed on me. Nevertheless, Mum booked the appointment, which felt like an eternity away.

It took so long to get an appointment I had no choice but to persevere with these foreign objects on my chest. Finally, my appointment came with the surgeon. My surgeon was local at Castle Hill, NSW, and he was an older man. I was somewhat nervous and the youngest person in his busy waiting room and all my brain power was focused on was how was I going to show this man my breasts?

I went to my appointment, and we chatted for some time with the surgeon; he was so lovely. I spoke much more than I had at the GP. He had a caring nurse who helped tremendously in making me feel comfortable. The nurse assisted with the physical examination and was very prompt in drawing the curtain, taking photos, giving me coverage and maintaining my dignity.

The surgeon explained what a breast reduction was and the risk with my age. Being under the age of 18 (I was 16 at the time), he was very reluctant to perform such drastic surgery. I was very persistent that this was what I wanted more than anything in the world. I insisted I would never have children, give away a kidney to not have to wear bras designed for 60 yrs+ women and quit dancing after over 10 years of attending a performing arts school.

This was not aesthetic surgery; my entire life was dependent on having this surgery. I am sure he thought I was crazy, but for a 16-year-old girl, isolated from the world, trapped in a body she hated, it was all I wanted. It was, for me, soul-destroying. So, the surgeon booked us back in, gave us homework, and sent us off to read.

After reading and understanding, my mum and I went back to the surgeon. It was agreed I would have liposuction to the breasts. The countdown for this was elating. I went to the same private hospital on the day of surgery that I attended as an emergency patient. This time was very different, and I was full of excitement and hope. I had the surgery and was left in bandages.

I learnt that I did love myself; I loved so many qualities I have and the achievements I made. I did not love my breasts; I did not view them as part of me. The surgery was only very short and the recovery was very easy. But for me psychologically and getting through that period of my life, the surgery truly saved my life.

I regained my confidence, freedom and friends. I became the happy, bubbly and ambitious child my parents had lost. I was back to being a massive pain in the ass. I also went on to have four children and breastfed for over five years; it turned out that the specialist plastic surgeon did have some insight and was indeed right. Had it not been for him, I wonder if I would have ever had children or lived the fulfilling life I have had so far.

The reason I wanted to share this very personal story was because I have never viewed cosmetic surgery as frivolous or simply aesthetic. So many people immediately judge those who do or don't have surgery, who admit they do or deny they did. I believe every patient is different, and every patient has the right to choose what they want to share.

I do not openly share my story; in fact, I never have in such detail to anyone. I have chosen not to share my story until now. I want to be as transparent as possible in this chapter; I want to scream from the rafters: Having aesthetic surgery does not mean you do not love yourself. Having aesthetic surgery is more than skin deep and is life-changing for millions of people around the world, from the very young to the very old.

Fast forward to now, and I wish I could say I practised what I preach. After having four children, I medically and aesthetically need an abdominoplasty. However, I have 101 excuses as to why I have not had one. I have this inert voice telling me a good mother spends all her money on her children. It is too expensive and indulgent. I cannot rest for the recovery time. I need to lose weight. Everyone around me will think I am selfish, vain and superficial.

45 is a real turning point for women; it is an age where I have heard thousands of patients say, *'I wish I did this earlier,'* in relation to both surgical and nonsurgical procedures. It is an age where you start to realise ageing is a privilege.

Ageing without illness is the greatest blessing. This is why I really do not like the terms 'anti-ageing' and 'youthful'. Why would anyone not want to age? If you are not ageing, you are dying or dead. A 45, 50- or 60-year-old woman wanting to look like a 20-year-old is concerning. I suspect the reason is to be perceived as sexy, to reclaim lost years and because you do not truly love and appreciate your age.

A 45+ woman wanting to look her best for her age is remarkable and sexy. Aesthetic treatments are not about looking like your early 20s, and if you are having a procedure at 45+ to look like a 20-year-old, you will likely be constantly disappointed.

If you are having a procedure to change your unique essence, quirks and physical look completely, what will make you unique? More importantly, what do you love about yourself? If the answer is nothing, then the core issue is much deeper and cannot be simply solved with a needle or knife. Aesthetic treatments, surgical or nonsurgical, are not medical, which means they are not deemed as necessary.

However, as with my earlier story, they can have a profound impact on someone psychologically. This is why I would argue there are many instances whereby they are medical.

In any case, the guilt never ends for women. We are guilty when we spend too much and invest in ourselves. We are guilty that we do not look our best selves and become fiercely angry if we see our partners checking out the younger, sexier women who clearly do take care of themselves.

Sometimes, I look at women my age and feel so inferior. I think, goodness, how do they look so good? Trim, taught, clear complexions and perfect symmetry. Being in this industry, I go straight to the inner voice, *'They've had a lot of work done.'*

Then I must catch myself and remind myself, *'Nicole, you are being a judgemental biatch.'*

Whether they have or haven't had work done is none of my business. For argument's sake, if they have, good on them for investing in themselves.

We are taught we "should" love ourselves; however, we were born is how we were meant to be. Our hereditary hump nose, or ears which stick out, pencil-thin lips or a gummy smile. The list could go on and on with all the unique traits we have, which are not a reflection of what we see online when looking at celebrities and superstars.

As a parent, it is even harder, as we want our children to love themselves no matter what. Meanwhile, they have social media telling them everything wrong with themselves. Young girls are desperate to have huge invasive surgery as soon as they turn 18. Most often, they are scared to tell their parents.

I have spoken to many labiaplasty patients who would never share with their parents they had this huge surgery. These patients feel their parents would say, *'You are perfect the way you are,'* and encourage self-love.

At some point, this philosophy of loving yourself becomes toxic. Making people feel ashamed of their self-loathing can be very isolating. Not only do you have an insecurity you want to amend or alter, but you have the compiled guilt from society and yourself.

When our children look at influencers, celebrities and their idols and we say, *'But they are famous,'* it creates this us-and-them-mentality – they are different because they have chefs, personal trainers and plastic surgeons. It's nearly like saying they are worthy, wealthy and better than us.

They are revered for their beauty on a pedestal regardless of what they have or have not done aesthetically. We have no clue if that celebrity has body dysmorphia, which is highly likely in some cases. Especially when we see those where actors or celebrities have gone too far; they lose work and can be unrecognisable. When the tabloids share what they may or may not have had done, we all jump on and judge them, thus making ourselves feel better.

As if they only look that good because of surgery or lots of expensive treatments. Disregarding the hard work, rejection, guilt, pain and sacrifices they may have made to be able to access and go through with the procedure. Many procedures are painful, have considerable downtime and can be a tough journey psychologically and physically.

On the flip side, we have more and more women and men having procedures you would never know about, from anti-wrinkle injections to full-body surgery. Whatever the reason is, it is a personal journey.

Every person deserves the right to feel good about themselves. To not feel guilty for investing in themselves. To feel unique, special and most importantly, to love themselves for all their inherited genes – good bad and dare I say, ugly. Our perception of beauty is as unique as beauty itself, which is why we need to support each other and each other's choices.

When people, especially children, can speak openly in a safe space and feel supported, magic happens. Our inner voice is so powerful and it is not easy for anyone on the journey of ageing, self-acceptance and self-love.

It has taken me over 20 years within the beauty/aesthetic industry to realise that what you look like never attracts or detracts from friends, love, employment, or opportunities. It is our energy and feelings towards ourselves.

To truly appreciate the breasts that are too big or small but feed four children. The nose that is too wide and will never be a button. Whatever it is for you is what makes you – you.

If you want to invest in your body, preserve and enhance your uniqueness, do so without guilt and out of love because you deserve to feel your best every day.

ROVE
CREATIVE

KATE SMITH

❝ Everything we need is already inside of us. ❞

Chapter Eleven

KATE SMITH

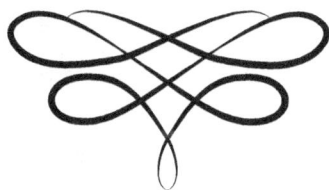

I gave in to the beautiful chaos. Arms brushing mine, someone else's hair momentarily across my face, a near miss with someone's stiletto and my toes, my partner's intense gaze, monitoring the space around us. I stopped worrying that I wasn't the best dancer in the room. I let the joy of the movement rise through me and out into those around me. I smiled at the startled woman whose partner nearly led her into us, caught the eye of my friend across the room, smiling back at me and grinned at my partner as we pulled off a complicated turn pattern.

The world smiled with me. Nothing else mattered but this move and the next one and the next, driven by my dance partner leaving me in the bliss of the moment, no need to think, just to flow.

Later, ascending a bridge, I watched the lights sparkle off the still water. I pedalled madly and then let the bike swoop back and forth playfully on the way down. There were no hills in Osaka, so you had to take advantage of any freefall you could find. Still mercilessly happy, I smiled at some young salarymen as I passed, then heard one of them call out a heavily accented *'I love you!'* behind me. The kind of catcall you can't be mad at. I laughed out loud, flashed them a smile and kept riding.

It wasn't the first time I'd been told that in the street, late at night, when copious amounts of alcohol had lowered Japanese inhibitions sufficiently to speak to a foreigner. It seemed one of the few English phrases people reliably knew. I found it strangely beautiful but sad, as it was a phrase that was seldom used among Japanese people, even married couples, but called to a stranger in a rare moment of self-permission.

I asked myself what I always ask after dance, *'How do I bottle this feeling?'*

This invincibility, this pure joy, this feeling that I was good and beautiful and I inspired others to love and be happy just by being – how do I feel like this all the time?

One week later, I was as far away from that feeling as possible. I sat out the front of the hostel I ran and lived in. It was nestled between love hotels on the border of Tennoji Park. Couples wandered by surreptitiously, whispering sweet nothings to each other.

I sighed into the beer I was sipping. Bedbugs. I felt sick. Not because of the bugs – although that was icky enough. But because I was sure my staff were all going to abandon ship, the owner was going to take no responsibility and I was going to be left with cleaning mattresses and explaining this to guests by myself.

I'd built such a team, such a little bubble of friendship and comradery. A safe haven for travellers from all parts of the world and all walks of life. But it was all going to fall apart. If I were a volunteer in a bedbug-infested hostel, I'd be out of there like a flash!

Pedro, one of my staff, stood up, *'I'm heading to bed.'*

I called goodnight, then stood and said the same to the last man standing. He was a tradie from Australia – I'd checked him in an hour ago for two nights. His response startled me.

'No, you're not, we're going to talk about you now. What's wrong?'

This was the last thing I'd expected to hear! I mumbled, *'Nothing is wrong,'* pretty noncommittally and not without defensiveness. *'Goodnight.'*

Five hours later, with the sun coming up, I sat there smiling and in tears. He'd dragged the whole story from me and proceeded to give me a solution. He'd spent hours with me, giving me scenarios and asking questions about how my body felt.

'Imagine you're in your favourite outfit, the one that makes you feel a million dollars. How do you feel? Where do you feel it? What colour is it? Where does it start and where does it go?'

At first, my answers were reserved. This was so foreign to me. Not to mention that it seemed completely irrelevant.

'What's your favourite thing to do?' he queried.

'Dance.'

'Okay. Imagine you are dancing. Think of the music, the light, your movement, who is around you, the colours and objects in the space. Bring the scene to life. Do you see it?'

'Yes.'

'Are you happy? Does this feel like a yes?'

'Yes.'

'Where is the feeling? Is it moving? Is it fast or slow? Does it expand or contract? Is it bright or dark? How does it move?'

He encouraged me to vocalise all my answers. To explain this feeling in my body to him.

Finally, I could define it as white light, moving up and expanding from my solar plexus and heart to the sky. A sort of V shape that kept expanding. I needed to sit straight and upright to properly feel it. When I visualised it, I felt the joy. That feeling I wanted to bottle. He'd shown me how! He called this my 'Yes'.

We did the same process for my feeling of 'No' until I could feel that clearly in my body too, visualise it and explain it.

'It's like a hard rock in my solar plexus, dark red, rough and bumpy, heavy,' I observed.

'Now you have your No and your Yes, you're going to do an exercise every day, three times a day. How long do you think you can sustain your Yes feeling, one minute? Three minutes, 10? Okay, three. Three times a day for three minutes. Go somewhere you won't be disturbed. You're going to visualise the hostel as you love it, with your staff happy and joking around, everything running smoothly and just like you want it. And bring your Yes feeling to that. Your problems will be gone in a week. But in just three days, you won't even feel like you have problems.' he instructed.

I didn't believe him. Why had I stayed up all night doing this craziness with a stranger?

'Tell a friend to keep you accountable. You don't have to tell them what you're doing. Just get them to ask you, 'Have you done the thing today?''

Without a better idea of what to do, I asked Gerben, the sweet and thoughtful Dutchman who used to work for me and now stayed as a guest long-term, studying music and Japanese. I always opened karaoke night with *'Hotel California'*. Those who knew, knew. He agreed and asked no questions.

Three days later, my staff were on board and dedicated to eradicating what they had dubbed 'the curse'. The meditation had brought the team closer and given them a common goal, the reaching of which benefited us all. It gave me the fuel to lead in a way that lent us all confidence we could do this.

I didn't realise then what a gift Rob the Sparky had given me.

I use the exercise whenever I have a problem that I can't logically find a solution for. But knowing my Yes and my No, being conscious of that is something that has guided me when I let it. When I have a decision to make and I don't know what to do, I give myself the possible scenarios, tune into my body and see if I feel a Yes or a No. It seems so irrational, and there is nothing to base important decisions on or rely on. I *still* need to remind myself to trust this. But it's never led me down the wrong path.

~

It was cold. I sat on the back deck, where some weak sunlight seeped through the lattice. The sagging couch and coffee table made a poor workspace, but my hands were aching from the frigid air in my office. How is it that Queenslander houses are colder on the inside than out?

I read the brief again. It was a fashion app for teenagers and 20-somethings. Complete website redesign, app redesign and brand restyle. I was in over my head. I had quoted as my coach had instructed. He'd made me raise my rates and quoting now gave me heart palpitations.

Kate Smith

And they'd said yes.

I was in disbelief. And horrified. How was I meant to create thousands of dollars of value for these people? Why had they trusted me to do this? *Paid* me to do this? Because a lovely young woman I met at a networking group referred me. She thought I could do it, and now they thought I could do it. But they didn't know me! I actually felt like I couldn't breathe all the way into my lungs.

I couldn't do this. It was too big. It was too much.

In the old gum off the back deck, a kookaburra cackled into derisive laughter. It should have been kind of funny, but it made me want to cry. I was one step away from full-blown panic. I took a gulp of cold tea and set it back on the coffee table. I picked up my phone and put it down again. Picked it up again and texted my coach, *'Dale, any chance you've got time for a call?'*

And it was fashion! I had never been trendy; I'd tried when I was younger but always fell short of the mark. I'd evolved into my own quirky style, which people probably thought was weird. All my clothing was thrifted. I was *not* the right person to do this job.

My phone rang, *'Hey Dale.'*

'What's up?'

'I think I should give this deposit back and tell them I can't do this rebrand.'

171

As I heard what I said, I knew how stupid it sounded to him. This project was everything we'd been working towards. *'I'm just not able to do a good enough job for what they're paying.'*

My voice shook and I fought to hold it together. This man didn't need to hear me cry. Again. Poor Dale. He must regret ever taking me as a client.

I heard him sigh on the other end of the phone line but kindly without exasperation. *'What part of this feels hard?'*

'Well, it's fashion and I don't know anything about that. And the website is huge, there's so much to figure out there. I can't do it.'

In my mind I added, *'If I try, they're going to figure out I'm a fraud, that I've taken their money but I'm no good.'*

I was six weeks into full-time business ownership, though I barely had enough work to keep me busy 20 hours a week, and I didn't feel like I owned very much.

'And have you branded other types of businesses that you don't know about before?'

'Well, yes. But they-'

'And have you restructured websites before?'

'Not as big as this-'

'So, you can do it because you've done it before. Right?'

Kate Smith

Stop being so logical! *'Yes, but it's not going to be good enough.'*

'Go through the process Kate, do your research, just like you would any other project. They're not paying crazy money. That's just what these services cost.'

Every minute of work I did on that project was excruciating. I had to physically hold myself in my seat. Every minute an impulse to put on a load of laundry or do some food prep or sweep the deck or water the plants popped into my mind. Focusing felt impossible. Why was I such an unmotivated, lazy piece of work?

I'd spent way too much time on this project, every moment of it with a knot in my stomach, feeling like an imposter, terrified I was wasting my time and theirs. But today was the deadline and it was 5pm.

I felt sick, but I hit send.

I walked out the door. Sunset beers at a riverside bar I couldn't afford should distract me. Damn my employed friends wanting to go to fancy places.

As I wandered through the tables, trying to spot my crew, I saw a table of young women, the oldest might have been 20, dressed in bright colours. Their outfits could have been painted with the colour palette I'd just submitted to my client. A little kernel of hope blossomed in my chest. I breathed into my diaphragm for the first time in days.

I pulled out my phone to call my friends, but they were nowhere to be seen. An email notification appeared on my home screen. The newfound space in my chest collapsed. I felt nauseous, but I opened the notification in sick fascination.

'We LOVE it, Kate!'

I went dizzy with relief; my whole body seemed to sag with outgoing tension.

'It's amazing, the colours, the style, we couldn't have imagined it would be this perfect! And I love how you've rearranged the site menu…'

I was interrupted by Dani hugging me, *'Hey, what's up?'*

'Nothing! Nothing at all.'

I couldn't believe how much pressure I'd put on myself, how little I'd believed in myself, how *sure* I was that I was USELESS. Where was my proof that I couldn't do this project? Now, it seemed easy with the effusive feedback in my pocket. But I vowed to question *everything* next time that showed up in my head.

I've experienced imposter syndrome many, many times since then. Every time it's debilitating, it never feels better. But I know now that it never lasts and is not the truth. My coach was instrumental in keeping me going through that bout. Now I know to reach out to friends whose opinions I trust and share this feeling. It's a form of shame and shame cannot survive connection. Their belief in me helps to bolster mine.

Self-inquiry has also been super powerful. Why does this feel hard? Why do I think I can't? Is this objectively true? What do I *know* I can do? When have I done something like this before?

Much later, someone told me, *'Imposter syndrome is a beautiful symptom of caring deeply. You wouldn't feel that way if that wasn't incredibly important to you.'*

If only I'd heard that all that time ago! Recognising this changes the energy. It's much more empowering, and I feel like I can give it the space and time it deserves. This feeling is here because I'm dealing with something important.

~

'Kate! They're looking for a graphic designer in my department. Come work with meeee!'

The message was followed by a link. Government role, list of things I could already do, great benefits, $100K salary.

It was midday Friday, and I was in Caloundra with a friend. I passed my phone to him.

He whistled, *'How much are you making now?'*

I made a noise halfway between a scoff and a sigh. My business had barely pushed above $30K last year. Deduct from that $5K for a coach and almost as much for a new laptop.

'Not that much.'

If not for the Self Employment Assistance Program, I would have had to go and work for someone else already. I hadn't paid myself any super and my list of duties included things I had no idea how to do.

My first year in business hadn't been very prosperous. Why *was* I busting my ass to live below the poverty line? Frantically trying to learn how to do sales and accounting and public speaking.

But if I had a regular job, could I be working from the beach on a Friday afternoon? We wouldn't have beaten the weekend traffic to have a swim before dinner and enjoy the evening. We would have been sitting in the campervan in traffic from 6-8pm.

But if I had a cushy government job, maybe I'd be staying in a nice Airbnb, not squished into a van and showering on the beach. I smiled to myself; I liked roughing it.

I applied anyway.

The relief was instantaneous. I'd surrendered all my responsibilities into the hands of some HR manager. If I got this job, I could relax. I wouldn't have to worry about where my next paycheck came from. I would never need to speak in front of a room full of entrepreneurs and pretend I was one of them again. I could throw *Xero* out the window and go back to doing a nice, simple tax return each year. Imagine not having to do another sales call? Ever!

But with the release of responsibility also came a deep sense of disempowerment. I'd failed. I couldn't do it. The self-employed, digital nomad, creative entrepreneur dream was done. I'd go back to a soul-crushing life of creating boring corporate layouts, sending them off into the ether, wondering who would see them, only to be told weeks later that the project had never gone ahead, so they weren't used.

But I would be financially secure. And that was important, right?

One year later, I was sitting in an apartment in Singapore. My 16-year-old cousin was sitting next to me; we were drawing. She'd asked what I did for work. She was currently navigating that phase of life where you think every move you make will affect the rest of your life. Well-meaning teachers and parents turning up the pressure to succeed in school, with the looming threat of some existential 'failure' ruining your life forever.

'Do you want to do some work with me?'

'Sure.'

So, we were drawing turtles. I was rebranding a travel agent who wanted to move into a more affluent market. They wanted to keep their turtle icon, but they needed to look high-end to appeal to people with money to burn on trips to Oceania. Then they could really flex their vast experience and expertise in creating once-in-a-lifetime holidays.

We explored different illustration styles, looked at turtle tattoos, and created technical drawings and simple line sketches, abstract shapes that almost wouldn't be turtles if you didn't want them to be. Later, I would digitise the most promising concepts to develop them into logo concepts and full brands.

A holiday brand, created on my holiday. Dreamy, right?

I'd been in Indonesia for the last month, working on the business more than in it, enjoying Balinese food, and doing a lot of yoga. I didn't want to leave, so I booked a quick jaunt to visit family in Singapore and re-entered Indonesia with a new tourist visa.

'What do you think of this?' my cousin asked, holding up her latest drawing. She was good.

'This is cool! I love this curve… What if you made his fin a bit more compact? That would make a finished logo easier for the client to use.' She smiled and went back to work.

What a beautiful opportunity to connect with family. An impossibility with a 'real job'. I'd be back at my desk right now, lamenting the 4-6 weeks leave I'd already used up. Recovering from a whirlwind holiday that had left me more drained than fulfilled.

I hadn't done anything special to get here. Just kept putting one foot in front of the other. In the end, I didn't have much other choice. I didn't get that government job.

So I kept struggling, making ends meet, making sales calls and getting more and more confident speaking to a room full of business owners. Things that were excruciating last year were normal to me now.

There are a lot of statistics thrown around at networking meetings about how many new businesses fail. When I first heard this, I thought it must be fatally flawed business plans or going bankrupt. But most businesses die by suicide. We give up. We go back to work and our little creation of individuality, our business, dies.

Business is a journey. A marathon. There are sprints, but it's the consistent effort over time that creates your vision. You will grow in ways you never imagined possible, meet people you didn't think existed and become more yourself every day as you take each step to build something that is for you.

It's not easy, but it's so, so worth it.

~

My takeaways from my short time in business are these:

Trust yourself. Your gut. Your heart. Your feeling is always right, no matter what logic might tell you. Bottle your joy and ask yourself what feels most like that.

Don't believe the negativity in your own head. Seek the opinions of others. Someone will always be there for you, whether for love or money. Sometimes, people will help you for no reason at all.

And above all else, don't give up. The journey of a thousand miles begins with the first stumble, and it's not even about reaching a destination. Enjoy the process and be in awe of where it takes you.

You've got this.

the Quiet COLLECTIVE

CASEY LIGHTBODY

❝ It's not about being a perfect parent or abandoning your ambitions. It's about being aware of the season you're in and making conscious choices about how you navigate it. ❞

www.quietcollective.com.au

Chapter Twelve

THE CYCLE OF MOTHERHOOD: FROM FULL NEST TO EMPTY NEST

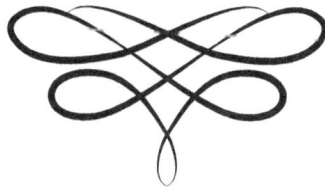

I'm sitting here in the swansong of my youngest child's final month of school before he graduates and I officially become an empty nester. It's a peculiar space to inhabit, this liminal moment between two significant life stages. For over two decades, my identity has been inextricably linked to being a mother of school-age children. Now, as I stand on the precipice of change, I find myself reflecting on how this season of my life has passed in what feels like the blink of an eye.

My mind drifts back to when I first became a mom in England. A house buzzing with three kids under six. It was beautiful chaos – skinned knees, bedtime stories, and so many questions.

So. Many. Questions.

'But Mom, can I ask you a question? Mom, I have a question! But why, Mom?'

It was incessant and sometimes, exasperating. But looking back now, I wouldn't trade it for the world. The memories made like the secret three-squeeze handshake that was code for 'I love you' with my youngest, or how my eldest would get all serious, bossing his younger brothers around for our homemade Easter and Christmas shows, or how our middle one would scrunch up his nose and blink like crazy when we were teaching him how to wink. Priceless.

Before I knew it, childhood morphed into the rollercoaster of teenage years. And then… BAM. Five years ago, reality struck! My eldest, just 17, left for the army. Oof, I can still feel the pang, even now. I can see it as clear as day: him packing his bags, giving our dog one last pat, and then wheeling his suitcase down the street to catch that bus to Wagga Wagga for his basic training. He looked so young to be setting out on his own and I was ill-prepared for the immense grief that followed.

From Full Nest to Empty Nest

Those early days after he left were harder than I could have imagined. Every time I walked past his room, it hit me all over again. The pandemic added another layer of complexity – unable to visit, prohibited from speaking to him on his 18th birthday due to the no-phone-contact rule, missing his passing out ceremony. Each 'no' felt like another little heartbreak.

You know, I've never really talked about those 10 months before. They were brutal, and looking back, I wish someone had given me a heads-up about how tough it would be.

And as if that wasn't enough, I kept hearing my mom's voice in my head: *'You lose your sons, but you never lose your daughters.'*

That saying always rubbed me the wrong way, hinting at a future where my relationship with my boys would be distant and strained.

But you know what? Five years down the road, I've realised how off-base that old saying was. My relationship with my eldest? We've got this amazing connection – he gets me, I get him. We chat every other day about everything from relationship drama to business strategies.

My middle son? That's a whole different ball game. While he's left school, he's still living at home, navigating the space between adolescence and full independence. And oh boy, do I cherish every moment that I have with him. I find myself trying to overlook the owl-like sleep patterns that turn our household rhythms topsy-turvy and the perpetually messy bedroom that seems to defy the laws of order and cleanliness. But his being here reminds me that this whole empty nest thing isn't always cut and dry. It's more like a slow dance with its own set of hiccups and high points.

And now, as I'm staring down this new chapter with my youngest, those old patterns of worry niggle at the back of my mind. What does the future hold? The uncertainty mingles with excitement for what's to come. And a tinge of regret, if I'm truthfully honest... But more to come on this.

So here I am, standing on the edge of this new chapter, feeling all sorts of things. There's a sense of accomplishment in having raised three children to adulthood, a twinge of sadness at the closing of this chapter of active, day-to-day parenting, but also a spark of excitement for what lies ahead for my kids, for me, and for how we'll keep growing together.

It's not my first rodeo when it comes to big life changes, you know? As I reflect on this whole motherhood journey, I'm reminded of another huge shift that turned our family's world upside down. 16 years ago, we jumped into something that would really put us through our paces, shake up everything we knew, and end up adding so much richness to our lives in ways we never saw coming. It was a decision that kicked off a whole new season of growing, adventuring and stumbling into opportunities we never expected.

The Seasons of Immigration: Uprooting and Replanting

16 years ago, my life took a dramatic turn. With three children under the age of six, my husband and I made the bold decision to immigrate to a brand new country – one where we had never even set foot before. It was scary, exciting and overwhelming all at once.

We were craving a lifestyle reminiscent of our African roots – wide open spaces, sunshine most of the year, and a laid-back culture. More than that, we wanted to create a future for our kids where they would feel at home, without the constant worry about relocation that had been part of our lives growing up in Africa. It was a big change, but one we felt was necessary for our family's future.

The day we arrived in Australia, the air felt different, the sounds unfamiliar, and the future uncertain. I'll never forget walking off the plane, trying to juggle a double buggy, three car seats, and five suitcases while keeping track of three small children. And then, as if the universe wanted to test us right off the bat, we were suddenly surrounded by police and sniffer dogs. In my haste to get everyone and everything off the plane, I'd forgotten to get rid of/declare a half-eaten apple buried in one of the kids' rucksacks. Talk about a welcome party, right?

Those early days were a whirlwind of activity and adjustment.

One day in that first week stands out vividly. My husband was away on business in Sydney, and I was camping out in our rental accommodation with makeshift furniture. Plastic knives and forks, paper plates, mattresses on the floor lent by our generous new neighbours, and bean bags for couches while we waited for our container to arrive from London.

I decided to brave a trip to the grocery store with all three kids in tow. Navigating unfamiliar brands and trying to figure out the difference between green and purple notes for payment was challenging enough. But it's what happened after I treated the kids to a $2 carousel ride that really shook me.

As we were leaving, I popped the youngest in the trolley, the six-year-old by my side, calling for the three-year-old who was always on his own mission. My heart nearly stopped when I realised he was nowhere to be seen. In a panic, I thrust the other two kids into the hands of a stranger and took off sprinting through the shopping centre, screeching for help. I was lost, didn't know where to go or who to reach out to, and felt utterly, utterly helpless.

Then it hit me – what the hell was I thinking, leaving two of my children with a complete stranger? I raced back, relief washing over me as I saw they were safe. And then, like a miracle, I saw another stranger walking towards us, holding my three-year-old's hand.

In that moment, I felt a mix of emotions I'll never forget – the sheer terror of losing a child, the guilt of leaving the others, and the overwhelming gratitude for the kindness of strangers.

That day encapsulated so much of what our early time in Australia was like – challenging, scary, but also filled with unexpected kindness. It was a time of profound change, where everything familiar was stripped away and we had to learn to navigate a whole new world.

Looking back, I can see how our immigration journey mirrored the cycles of nature. Leaving England was like autumn, a time of letting go. Those first confusing months felt like a harsh winter – unfamiliar and isolating. But as we began to settle in, make friends, and find our feet, it was like spring was slowly arriving. New opportunities bloomed, the kids started to thrive, and we began to feel the warmth of belonging in our new home.

The Business Lifecycle: From Seed to Harvest

As we settled into our new life in Australia, a long-held dream began to resurface. Even back in England, I'd dabbled in business, driven by a desire to create something beyond motherhood. Now, with my youngest starting *kindy* in this new country, it felt like the perfect time to nurture that seed of entrepreneurship.

The leap of faith we'd taken in moving across the world had unknowingly prepared me for this next adventure. The persistence, flexibility, and courage I'd developed as an immigrant were about to serve me well in a completely different arena: the world of business. Little did I know that this new journey would challenge and reshape me just as profoundly as our international move had.

I can still remember the mixture of excitement and terror when I took that first leap. Without a website, logo, or really any plan at all, I agreed to help a fellow school mom with her marketing. It was exhilarating and terrifying all at once, reminiscent of watching my children take their first wobbling steps – uncertain, but full of possibility.

That initial venture grew rapidly, transforming from a one-woman marketing consultancy into an agency with a team of five. Sounds great, right? But I guess, the lesson here is to be careful what you wish for. Because the reality was that instead of the freedom I'd dreamed of, I was tethered to my desk 24/7, drowning in work.

Life was being sucked out of me. I didn't see it at the time, but I felt it. The exhaustion. The overwhelm. The frustration. The irony wasn't lost on me – I'd created a business to have more time with my kids, and now I was missing so many special moments, trying to be present but, in fact, completely distracted or absent.

In a moment of clarity – or perhaps desperation – I made the decision to burn that business to the ground. The relief was palpable, but so was the fear. What would come next?

What followed was a period of soul-searching that would make *Eat, Pray, Love* look like a casual weekend getaway. I dug deep, peeling back layers I didn't even know I had. And you know what I found? An introverted, highly sensitive woman who'd been wearing an extrovert mask for so long she'd forgotten her own face.

This realisation led to a new venture, one that felt so much more authentic. I set out to help other introverted, sensitive women create businesses that felt like home. No more hustle culture, no more 'fake it 'til you make it'. Just authentic, sustainable success on our own terms. It was more than a business; it was a mission. And I poured my heart and soul into it.

I often jokingly referred to my business as my 'baby girl', a nod to the fact that I had three sons but no daughters. This metaphor was more apt than I initially realised – because like a child, this business also required constant attention, nurturing, and adaptability.

It's been a constant juggling act for me personally, trying to navigate building a business with being a mom. And the cycles of this business mirrored the seasons of motherhood in ways I never expected. There were exhilarating growth spurts that left me breathless and periods of drought that had me questioning everything.

One of those highs came when I least expected it. Here I was, standing on stage, knees knocking, about to present to a room of people, focused on overcoming my fear of public speaking. I had no expectations – I was literally just showing up and sharing everything I knew.

Somehow, some way, I walked away from that event with $100,000 worth of sales. The kicker? I closed the final sale from my bed because I caught COVID-19 at the conference. Talk about a rollercoaster! People told me I was the most genuine person in the room and how much they got from my presentation. The high was indescribable; a validation that I was on the right path.

But for every high, there was a low that had me questioning everything. I remember hosting my first virtual summit. I'd interviewed world-famous speakers, my desk covered in sticky notes, nerves jangling as I wondered if I'd done a good enough job. I held my breath when I launched it, having no idea what to expect. The result? Over 4,000 attendees and exactly zero sales. Zero. It was a humbling experience, to say the least. I wanted to crawl into bed and never come out.

During these lows, the doubts would creep in. Was it worth continuing? Should I throw in the towel? Was this just some crazy, unrealistic dream? And truth be told, I had a lot of external voices telling me so. But if there was one thing that immigration taught me, it was persistence and resilience. So I kept going, kept showing up.

This journey has been a constant juggling act, trying to balance building a business with being a mom. There were times when I felt I was failing at both. But as my children grew, so did my business, and I feel like I have so many lessons to share as I enter my 'Crone era'.

The Wisdom of Cycles: Lessons for the Next Generation

As I stand on the threshold of this new chapter, poised to embrace my Crone era, I reflect on the intricate dance of motherhood, immigration, and entrepreneurship that has shaped my life. It's a dance of seasons, of ups and downs, of growth and consolidation. And let me tell you, it's been one hell of a ride.

From Full Nest to Empty Nest

I've had times when my business was on fire, with revenue flowing in faster than I could keep track. Exciting? Absolutely. But also utterly overwhelming. I imagine it like this: running a marathon in flip-flops, desperately trying to keep pace. The business is growing at warp speed. But you? Your leadership? Who you are as a person? These need to evolve overnight. Your mind and body? They're screaming for a break, struggling to adapt to this new reality. It's like being thrust into the driver's seat of a *Formula 1* car when you've just mastered a bicycle.

But here's the crazy part – and it took me years to figure this out – those overwhelming moments are pure gold. They're not setbacks; they're setups for your next level of growth. It's like the universe is tapping you on the shoulder, saying, *'Hey, time out. Let's make sure you're ready for this next big leap.'*

When things seem to plateau, that's not stagnation - it's integration. It's your chance to catch your breath, to let your newfound knowledge sink in, to allow your skills to solidify. Think of it like this: you've climbed to a new altitude and now, your body needs time to climatise. Your roots are digging deeper; your foundations are reinforcing themselves. You're not standing still; you're building the launchpad for your next quantum leap.

I've learned to cherish these moments of apparent stillness. They're the quiet before the storm of your next big breakthrough. So when you hit that plateau or dip, don't panic. Embrace it. Use it. Because that's where the magic of real, lasting growth happens.

And through this journey, I've learned another crucial, often heart-wrenching lesson: the power of patience. Oh, how

I've struggled with this one! As an ambitious, type A, driven woman this has been tough. But what I've learned is that in business, as in parenting, results rarely happen overnight. It's the 1% improvements, the small, consistent efforts that add up over time.

I recall the early days of my business when progress seemed painfully slow. The nights I spent staring at the ceiling, wondering if I was crazy to keep pushing forward. The moments of doubt that crept in, whispering that maybe I wasn't cut out for this after all. It was tempting to push harder, to force growth, to make something, anything happen.

But slowly, painfully, beautifully, I learned that sustainable success, like a healthy plant, needs time to establish strong roots before it can reach for the sky. It's a lesson that brought me to tears more than once and tested my resolve and faith in myself. Yet, this hard-won patience has served me well in all aspects of life – in nurturing my children through their own struggles, in adapting to a new country when homesickness threatened to overwhelm me, and in building a business that truly aligns with my values, even when it meant taking the longer, less glamorous path.

Through this journey, I've come to understand a profound truth:

Savour every moment because time is the one thing you can never get back.

As I alluded to earlier, this realisation hits me with an intensity that takes my breath away. A bittersweet longing washes through me – to turn back the clock, just for a day, to relive those precious moments that seemed so ordinary at the time.

To the young mothers out there, juggling careers and kids, dreams and diapers, I say this with all the love and urgency in my heart: Slow down. Be present. The emails can wait. The laundry can wait. But your children's childhood? That waits for no one. Remember, this is a season – a fleeting, beautiful season of having your kids at home. It may feel endless now, with its constant demands and sleepless nights, but I promise you, it passes in the blink of an eye.

This season is unique and filled with moments that will never come again. The first steps, the school plays, the bedtime stories… These are the threads that weave the tapestry of your family's life.

It's not about being a perfect parent or abandoning your ambitions. It's about being aware of the season you're in and making conscious choices about how you navigate it. It's about finding those small moments of connection amidst the chaos. It's about realising that sometimes, the most important business meeting of your day might just be a tea party with stuffed animals.

Because one day, you'll blink, and that noisy, messy, beautiful season of life will be over. The house will be quieter, cleaner, and you'll find yourself longing for the chaos you once wished away.

While you can't stop time, you can make sure that when you look back, your heart is full of memories, not regret.

AFTERWORD

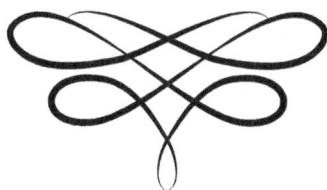

Birthing this book has been such a wild ride. There have been tremendous highs and challenging times as I ride the wave of stepping into a new identity and new age and co-creating and coaching my co-authors through their first authoring experience.

As with life, some of the ladies breezed through, while others took a little longer and needed an extra bit of tender loving care as they embarked on a massive transformation within their journey of becoming authors.

It takes an undeniable amount of courage to step up and say *'YES'* when the Wounding is screaming *'NO!'* constantly reminding you, *'You don't deserve this… You're not smart enough… Someone else can do it better… Your story isn't unique enough… What will people think when they find out about the real you? Will I fit in? Will it be good enough? Who am I to become an author? You're an imposter!'*

While you're almost silent Whisper, slowly and deliberately breezes in and out with its fleeting but fulfilling certainty.

I am forever grateful to the ladies who heard, listened, and trusted their Whisper in saying yes to sharing their personal experiences of the seasons and cycles of their lives and businesses and the highs and lows of life that have led each of them to where they are today.

I recommend taking a moment to follow each of my co-authors and reaching out to them and letting them know how their chapter has impacted your life, spoken to your heart, or simply added value to your life.

You will find that you resonate with some more than others, and that is exactly how it should be. One of my gifts is connecting incredible, high-calibre women through the pages of my books, inspiring spaces at my retreats, and the education and embodiment in my *Queens Club Business Mastermind*.

The feedback I get is that I am one of the best in the industry at this, and it truly fills my heart with joy each time either I or one of my products connects all the right people.

So, if you are a woman in business looking for a powerful, present, kind, caring community with unshakeable integrity and incredible people, please reach out so we can welcome you with open arms into a well-established and evolving group of change makers, healers and connectors with big hearts and even bigger visions.

Afterword

Please reach out to me personally to learn more about our *Aligned Woman Academy*, which is the perfect place to start as we combine community with content and connect powerhouse women from all over the world.

Through the pages of this book and over the past several years in business, I have laughed hysterically, cried uncontrollably, and had goosebumps on my skin as I witnessed and facilitated a homecoming for women.

Beautiful ladies, whether it's through the words in this book, attending a retreat, joining us in the *Aligned Woman Academy*, or being lucky enough to work with us 1:1 in the *Queens Club*, it's time to honour and educate yourself on the season and cycle of your life RIGHT NOW and align your life and business, choosing goals, thoughts, feelings, and actions that reflect that.

Let your Whisper lead the way so you can live your dream life, get paid to do what you love, with who you love, and set yourself up for long-term sustainable success that will last the test of time.

Remember that it doesn't feel good all the time, and if you are a woman devoted to her mission, purpose, parenting, and creation, there will be times of deep questioning, decay, and despair. There will be internal dialogue that will have you question every inch of your being and identity. There may even be times you question your own sanity or whether or not something is fundamentally wrong with you.

My hope for this book is that together, we have given you a framework, language, and community to discuss and share the natural seasons and cycles of a woman's life and overcome the shame and secrecy of a stolen and dismissed rite of passage into authentically aging women in society and business.

As we age, it is my hope that we undertake this rite of passage with the utmost reverence and respect for ourselves and each other rather than allowing ourselves to lose our value.

The content and the co-authors of this book have changed my life, and I dearly trust that they can change yours, too.

All my love,
Diane McKendrick

ABOUT THE AUTHOR

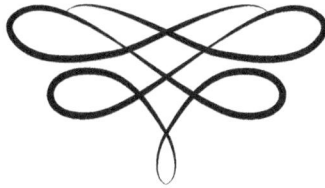

Diane McKendrick was born and raised in Ipswich and to this day, still resides in Ipswich, Queensland, Australia.

She is the second eldest of four. Born second to Michelle, her older sister by three years, Diane then graced the world with her presence. Allan was born a few years later and then Andrew joined the family two years after. The awesome foursome are still best friends, business partners and each other's biggest cheerleaders.

A small town girl with a big heart, she was a gifted athlete and by the time she was 17, Diane had represented her state and country both swimming and running.

Due to an injury, her direction and focus changed: as an 18 year old, Diane decided to escape the 'expectation' of going to university and backpacked around the world for two years.

Being of a naturally shy and timid nature, those two years abroad were very exhilarating, frightening and challenging.

Upon returning to Australia, Diane got a job as a receptionist at a shopping centre, spending the next 10 years working her way up to Portfolio Manager of several shopping centres.

She was about to move to Sydney to start her new job when she met a man with 'blue as the sea' eyes on the beach on Australia Day and chose her heart over her head. She decided to remain in Brisbane and married her husband Gus in 2010.

In 2012, Ross was born, then Esme popped out on the lounge room floor a few years later. Thanks to Alex from New Life Midwifery for the natural, magical home birth experience.

Today, Diane lives in Ipswich with her young family and is close to her extended family.

She has published four Best-Selling books, created online courses and run high-end luxurious retreats for businesswomen who are changing the paradigm of business.

The *Aligned* WOMAN Academy

An online school for women ready to stop PRETENDING and start LISTENING.
Supporting you to listen to YOUR whispers and live as the woman you were BORN TO BE

INCLUSIONS:

- Bi- Monthly Group Live Calls : Engage with Coaches and peers twice a month for in depth discussions and Q&A sessions
- Weekly Accountability: Receive weekly prompts and exercises to keep you on track and engaged.
- Highly Engaged Supportive Community
- Welcome Pack: Enjoy a gorgeous welcome pack that includes a copy of Diane's 3rd book (The Aligned Woman's Way), your own personalised journal, branded Those2Sisters pen, a bag of cacao and a bag of protein.
- Access to the monthly Coaching Couch Webinar
- Exclusive Resources: Access a wealth of tools, templates and guides.

UPGRADE and also receive a ticket to our next retreat

Aligned Woman Academy

SCAN ME

MOTIVATIONAL SPEAKERS

MICHELLE DIANE

TOPICS

- Lose your BUT (Your Fears)
- Embracing Uncertainty & Change
- Resilience
- Stress Management
- Self Care/Work-Life Balance

SISTERS ON A MISSION

We are Diane and Michelle. Yes we are REAL SISTERS on a mission to ignite change!

Diane, a former athlete and overachiever... Michelle a Science degree holder, full time coach and single Mum of 2.

Together we are here to support your audience to lose their BUT – that thing that has been holding them back - their FEAR.

We use our signature "Brain Body Being" model to have people completely change their outlook on life.

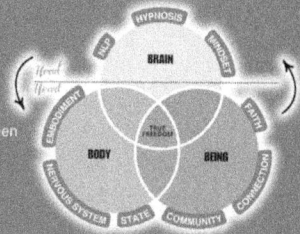

We have grappled with doubt and fear ourselves - Michelle, a single mother providing for her family in unprecedented times and Diane stepping up after her husband lost his international airline pilot job during COVID.

Our journey is a testament to the resilience found in embracing fear and surrendering to possibility.

We have charisma, energy and spark.

We will not only bring life long changes to your audience but everyone will leave with a smile and a spring in their step!

LESS Fear MORE Fulfilment.

LINKTREE

LINKTR.EE/THOSE2SISTERS

f facebook.com/Th0se2sisters

instagram.com/those2sisters_

in linkedin.com/company/those2sisters/

connect@those2sisters.com

NOTES

Notes

www.ingramcontent.com/pod-product-compliance
Lightning Source LLC
Chambersburg PA
CBHW030508210326
41597CB00013B/834